Contact

I CAREFULLY SLID my human flesh across the top portion of the alien's outstretched hand until my fingers folded over its outer edge. My thumb and index finger selected the outer digit on the alien's hand and explored its length, all the way down to the tapered end where my thumb made an unexpected find. At the tip was something like a fingernail, but the arched contour of the nail caused me to think that I was touching a claw, and then fear instantly flooded my mind.

My God, what is at the other end of this hand? That question was the only thought I could manage, as an image of the alien's form took shape. Abruptly, the contact ended, and my hand plopped down onto the bed.

I opened my eyes and sat up to look around the room. The aliens were gone. The time was 1:14 a.m.

My heart was still pounding, but the fear and panic that had come over me were rapidly draining away. What remained was a sense of amazement and the thrill of having experienced something close to a miracle.

"They let me touch them," I said to myself. "They actually let me touch them."

About the Author

Janet Bergmark is a training consultant and instructional designer in the Midwest, writing and producing corporate training materials for local, national and international companies.

To Write to the Author

If you wish to contact the author or would like more information about this book, please write to the author in care of Llewellyn Worldwide and we will forward your request. Both the author and publisher appreciate hearing from you and learning of your enjoyment of this book and how it has helped you. Llewellyn Worldwide cannot guarantee that every letter written to the author can be answered, but all will be forwarded. Please write to:

Janet Bergmark
c/o Llewellyn Worldwide
P.O. Box 64383 Dept. K063-9,
St. Paul, MN 55164-0383, U.S.A.

Please enclose a self-addressed, stamped envelope for reply, or $1.00 to cover costs. If outside the U.S.A., enclose international postal reply coupon.

IN THE PRESENCE OF ALIENS

Janet Bergmark

A Personal Experience of Dual Consciousness

1997
Llewellyn Publications
St. Paul, Minnesota 55164-0383

FIRST EDITION
First Printing, 1997

Cover design: Tom Grewe
Interior design and editing: Michael Maupin

Library of Congress Cataloging-in-Publication Data
Bergmark, Janet, 1955 -
  In the presence of aliens / Janet Bergmark. -- 1st ed.
      p.   cm.
  Includes bibliographical references.
  ISBN 1-56718-063-9 (pbk.)
  1. Human-alien encounters. I. Title
BF2050.B47   1997
001.942--dc21   97-25807
                                CIP

Llewellyn Publications
A Division of Llewellyn Worldwide, Ltd.
P.O. Box 64383, Dept. K063-9
St. Paul, MN 55164-0383, U.S.A.

Dedication

To Sheila
—cousin, confidante, and eternal friend—
whose gifts of curiosity, insight, and wisdom
have so often been my catalysts for change.

Contents

FOREWORD

PREPARE TO OPEN YOUR MIND. This story will take you beyond any other book on alien encounters.

Janet Bergmark's courage in writing this book is a testament that her experiences are real. Janet's decision to share her experiences is centered in her desire to help others who also may have experienced the phenomenon of alien contact.

Janet is a very intelligent, normal human being who has been faced with the challenge of making sense of often bizarre encounters with nonhuman life forms. Her story will challenge your perspective of reality. Can there be dimensions of reality beyond what our human senses perceive? Is there a gateway through our inner mind's soul consciousness? If there are such things as spirits, aliens, or angels, *what*, exactly, are they? And if you believe in angels, *where* would they be right now?

During the past ten years working in clinical hypnosis, I have found that many metaphysical concepts have been applicable to the healing processes of my clients. By looking within ourselves, we can find the answers and resources that are necessary to heal. Some of the concepts that emerged during Janet's encounters through hypnosis are regression, past life therapy, transdimensional travel and spirit attachment and releasement.

Hypnosis allows access to the subconscious mind. Located in the right brain, the subconscious mind houses habits, permanent memory, emotions, creative imagination, intuition, and spiritual consciousness. The subconscious maintains a profound level of communication and awareness to all parts of the physical body, regulating all the autonomic functions of the body, such as balance, breathing, and heart functions. This inner intelligence also seems to connect to our bio-energetic and soul essence energy. The soul essence is where knowledge of one's soul journey or past lives can be retrieved.

Hypnosis opens the door of communication to the inner mind, allowing hypnotic suggestions in the form of new ideas and concepts to enter—provided they are in harmony with our core inner beliefs. New ideas and concepts can replace negative thoughts or neutralize fear and anxiety associated with a traumatic event. Hypnosis, then, can create positive change by allowing the individual to move toward achieving desired goals.

Hypnotic regression allows knowledge from the subconscious to surface into a level of conscious awareness. The process of re-experiencing or reviewing places and past memories can enable a person to find insight, understanding, wisdom, and healing within his or her current life.

Past life therapy, also known as reincarnation therapy, is based upon the premise that our soul essence or life force energy holds energetic memories from other lifetimes. These memories may influence an individual's current life pattern. Reincarnation is the belief that our soul consciousness continues beyond death and incarnates into another physical embodiment. Returning to physical form allows the soul to continue its spiritual journey, learning to achieve oneness with God, or a higher being or higher source.

Transdimensional travel can take the form of an out-of-body experience, where an individual's consciousness separates from the physical body for a period of time. Or it can be accomplished through remote viewing, where the individual perceives people, places, and things across time and space. Hypnosis, too, creates an altered state of consciousness, sometimes freeing the inner mind to travel into other dimensional planes of existence.

Spirit releasement therapy is a process of clearing the influence or attachment of a disembodied consciousness that is the surviving consciousness of deceased humans or other dimensional beings such as an extraterrestrial consciousness. When a full or partial takeover of a living human occurs, this attachment is sometimes called spirit possession. Here, the inner mind seems to have awareness of these spiritual influences and can even achieve open communication with other levels of consciousness.

In the Presence of Aliens presents the reader with an unusual opportunity to perceive and explore these dimensions of inner consciousness. Like exploring the depths of the oceans or the reaches of outer space, new discoveries about our minds' potentials and abilities unfold.

Prepare now to open your mind and travel through an amazing journey of knowledge and healing that will connect you with a universal soul consciousness where all life forms may communicate and travel.

Gary Dallek
August, 1997

CHAPTER 1

"A Thousand Times Deeper"

ALL THE TINY MUSCLES, all the tiny nerves in and around your eyes are to become so relaxed that whenever I touch your hand you will go deeper, now." The hypnotherapist lightly tapped the back of my right hand, then paused for half a beat before continuing to speak. "As you go deeper, you breathe into the body. As you breathe out, each out-breath will continue to double the relaxation in your mind, as the sound of my voice circulates and mixes with each and every out-breath."

Sitting in a hypnotherapist's office was a totally new experience for me, one that induced a shifting mix of curiosity and concern. What will hypnosis feel like? How will I know when I'm under its effect? What will happen if I can't be hypnotized? I expected to feel some anxiety going into the hypnosis session—after all, I had never done this before—but I hadn't anticipated the swirl of excitement that marbleized the moment.

Fortunately, many of my questions about hypnosis were answered before my session began. Gary Dallek, the hypnotherapist, had carefully mapped out how the session would be conducted and explained what I could expect during the next hour and a half, saying, "At all times you will be conscious and fully aware of what is taking place here in the room. You will just be very relaxed."

I also had a positive attitude about hypnotherapy long before entering Mr. Dallek's small but comfortable office. A close friend had told me about her personal experience with hypnotherapy. It had enabled her to examine troubling memories and to gradually work through issues related to a childhood trauma. She emphasized that an important element in the success of her treatment was the trusting relationship she had developed with her therapist.

I knew as well that hypnotherapy had been successful in helping people with problems such as mine, a problem that was certain to be uncommon in any therapeutic setting. It was probably difficult to treat, too. That point alone was enough to convince me that I had to give hypnosis a try.

"As I count from ten down to one, each number will double the relaxation of your mind. The number five will take you a thousand times deeper, and the number one will double it again."

I squirmed to settle my form into the richly padded contours of the recliner beneath me, molding my arms and my legs into the beige leather upholstery while the weight of my skull carved out a soft hollow for my head. Every square inch of my body found a gentle place to rest and relax, and for a moment I knew only the experience of being in the chair, thinking that it was worth Mr. Dallek's hourly fee just to sit in his luxurious leather recliner. I felt firmly cradled and strangely pacified in the large chair, as if an invisible mist had descended and enveloped me in serenity.

More likely, it was the elevated levels of oxygen fanning my brain that was producing my tranquil state of mind; deep breathing would have that effect. But, whatever the reason, I barely noticed when the recliner leaned back and the footrest slid up under my calves.

"All things, all thoughts, all feelings, all sensations will move you deeper here today," I heard Mr. Dallek say. "As you go deeper, you become aware. You breathe into the body and go deeper, now. Ten. Gently and easily moving deeper, now."

With my eyes closed, I continued to listen to the slow, practiced melody defining the sound of Mr. Dallek's voice. Its smoothness, its steadiness bestowed the endless litany with an almost ceremonial charm. *Gently and easily moving deeper, now.* Such soft words, I thought as I repeated them to myself; soft, flowing words delivered with unquestionable confidence. But, of course, Mr. Dallek was a seasoned certified Master Hypnotist, a graduate of the Hypnotism Training Institute in Los Angeles, with a voice made for hypnosis. It was deep and resonant, a voice you could trust.

The first time I heard that voice was in April 1992. I had called Mr. Dallek after seeing his name in a course catalogue for the Open U, Inc., a local learning organization. He was teaching a class titled "Past Life Regression."

The course title, though, wasn't what caught my attention. What prompted a closer look was the fact that Gary Dallek was a professional member of the Association for Past Life Research and Therapies. I had heard of that particular association before, during a previous attempt to locate a hypnotherapist who could help me with my unorthodox problem.

That first attempt began with a phone call to the office of Dr. Edith Fiore, a clinical psychologist practicing in California. Dr. Fiore had written *Encounters*, in which she described how hypnotic regression enable many of her clients to examine memories of past events, even specific details buried in their subconscious minds. Through this technique, Fiore's clients were able to work through their fears and get on with their lives—something I desperately wanted to do.

I explained to an office assistant that I was calling to inquire if Dr. Fiore could possibly recommend someone in Minneapolis,

Minnesota, who was skilled in hypnotic regression. The assistant gave me the telephone number of the Association for Past Life Research and Therapies and added that the organization could provide me with a list of members practicing hypnosis in the Midwest.

With another phone call, and a few days later, I had that list in my hands. But after reviewing the members' credentials and personal profiles, I realized that the therapists whose names appeared on the list only applied hypnosis toward such goals as smoking cessation, weight control, and overcoming phobias. My specific problem was not mentioned, and the thought of calling any one of those practitioners and asking if they worked with people like me paralyzed my motivation to seek help. I couldn't imagine how I would explain my situation, and then there was the possibility that the therapist wouldn't even believe me.

Eventually, I threw the list away. I decided there had to be another way to find professional help—another route that would take me directly to someone not only skilled in hypnotic regression but who could also understand what was happening to me.

Several months disappeared, but my problem didn't. The symptoms I experienced continued to ebb and flow through my life, easing in the light of day, then flooding back during the night. The nights were always the worst. I would lie awake in my bed, unable to sleep because I was afraid to close my eyes, always wondering if I would ever find someone who could help me.

Miraculously, I did find someone.

I called Gary Dallek the same day I saw his name in the Open U catalog. I left a message on his answering machine, simply requesting that he return my call. Yet during the time I waited for Mr. Dallek to call me back, I almost called the whole thing off. I started thinking about how difficult—not to mention embarrassing—it would be to actually talk to someone about my problem.

But the telephone rang during a moment of courage, or maybe it was a moment of weakness brought on by the desperation I was feeling at the time and the realization that my personal efforts to deal with my sleepless nights, my anxiety, and my fear had failed repeatedly. Whatever the reason, I went ahead with my plan to seek professional help: I answered the call.

"What can I do for you?" Mr. Dallek asked, presenting the dreaded question.

I had actually rehearsed several versions of how I might explain my problem to Mr. Dallek in preparation for when he called. But when the phone finally rang, I still was uncertain of exactly what I would say. "I'm not quite sure how to tell you this because...well...because...I know it will seem really strange," I said, stumbling over my words, thinking that I must have sounded like a complete idiot.

"I'm sure that whatever it is, it will not surprise me," Mr. Dallek quickly offered. "I've heard many strange stories over the years."

Believing that I had nothing to lose at this point, I decided to just say it and get it over with. "I think...I think that I've had encounters with...with aliens," I finally admitted, taking a deep breath while waiting for Mr. Dallek's reply.

"Tell me about your experiences," he said.

I quietly sighed. What a relief it was not to hear him say, "You've got to be kidding," and it would have been even worse if there had been no response at all. Still, I couldn't help but wonder from how many people Mr. Dallek had heard the line "I think that I've had encounters with aliens." Probably not very many. But the sincerity in Mr. Dallek's voice told me he was truly interested in hearing about my experiences, and I knew that I would have to tell him about my encounters before he could help me. It was either now or later.

"Something happened to me when I was a teenager," I told him, after deciding to seize the moment. "I was around fourteen or fifteen years old."

The incident I described to Mr. Dallek over the telephone took place on a summer night in rural Wisconsin. I was babysitting for the Pritchards, a farm family who lived a few miles from the dairy farm where I spent the first eighteen years of my life.

During my early teens, I sat with the Pritchards' two children on a regular basis, which meant that I quickly became familiar with the children, the house, the entire babysitting routine. My experiences at the Pritchards' house were usually quite ordinary: I'd play with the children for a few hours, then see that they were cleaned up and in their beds by eight o'clock. But during one particular summer evening I participated in a series of events while at the Pritchards' that broke through the ordinary. What happened that night was something I would never forget.

A couple of hours after the children had been put to bed, I saw a bright light pass through the curtains drawn over the large picture window in the Pritchards' living room. That window permitted a view of the broad field that separated the house from the main highway. From where I had been sitting on the couch watching television, opposite the window, it appeared that the light might be headlights streaming across the field from a car moving up the long driveway.

I wondered if Mr. and Mrs. Pritchard might be returning home early for some reason. It was well before midnight, and I didn't expect them back for at least two hours or more. Still, I decided to unlock the side entrance to the house so they could let themselves in.

Earlier that evening, soon after the children were cleaned up and tucked in their beds, I had locked all the doors into the house, both the side and front entrances. Doing that was simply part of my babysitting routine. But later, the Pritchards' dog started barking, and that was not routine. In fact, the dog seldom made a sound.

Hearing the dog barking that evening grabbed my attention, particularly because the barking had that threatening tone dogs use when they are upset or frightened and serious about their intentions to keep someone or something away. The barking was fast, forced, and high pitched. It goaded my nerves enough to prompt an inspection to make certain that the doors to the house were actually locked. I found that they were.

After seeing the light stream through the picture window and thinking that the Pritchards were possibly returning from their evening out, I switched off the television and left the living room to unlock the side doors. As I walked out of the living room and into the kitchen, I listened for the sound of a car coming up the driveway. I heard nothing.

After unlocking the main door and the screen door, I walked back through the kitchen and into the living room to look out the picture window again. No lights were in sight, not on the main road or on the driveway. The lights had disappeared.

"Whatever I saw wasn't car lights," I said to myself, though puzzled about what could have caused the sudden illumination, as the light had been obvious and bright.

I returned to the side entrance and locked the doors again, and then went back to my place on the couch, where I paged through some magazines.

At least thirty minutes had passed when suddenly my concentration was pulled away from the magazine in my lap by a strange noise coming from an area just inside the side entrance to the house. It sounded like rustling or shuffling, like several bodies moving around in a small space. It was not the sound of someone opening a door; I never heard the screen door or the inside door ever being disturbed that night. But the sound that followed the shuffling noise was clearly recognizable, and under the conditions I faced that evening—being alone and responsible for the safety of two young children—that unmistakable sound sent an urgent message to my brain: an intruder was now in the house.

From where I sat on the couch, a wall separated me from the kitchen. It didn't close off the living room entirely, at least a five-foot opening remained. That opening exposed the dining area, which was located at one end of the kitchen. At the opposite end, a few steps led down to an entryway and to the side entrance with its two layers of doors.

I heard footsteps coming first from the entryway on the stairs, then, as a light impact on the kitchen floor. Someone, something was slowly walking through the kitchen and heading toward the opening to the living room, toward me.

Whoever, whatever was there moved cautiously, taking only a step or two at a time. Then, it would wait a few seconds before attempting another step.

In the meantime, I was sitting on the couch, staring forward, frozen in a state of disbelief. Though my eyes were wide-open, I doubt if I visually focused on anything during those moments. The only thing on my mind was the sound coming from the kitchen. I knew I was hearing footsteps; what I found hard to believe was why.

How did someone get into the house? I asked myself, knowing that the side doors were locked. There was no logic behind what my senses were telling my brain: Someone is walking through the kitchen, and whoever or whatever is there is now behind me, behind the wall, and heading toward the opening into the living room, toward me.

My bewilderment dissolved into fear, and it was fear that sent my pulse on a wild, wild race. In the next instant, a primal response gripped every muscle in my body, instinctively preparing it for action.

As soundlessly as possible I moved off the couch and into the middle of the room. Standing alone, still listening with fear-focused intensity, I fixed my gaze upon the right edge of the opening to the kitchen, toward the direction of the faint but discernible footfalls. I knew that whoever, whatever was moving toward me was now just a few feet away, and that realization left me petrified. Time slowed, and each protracted second brought the intruder closer to where I stood waiting, heart-pounding, barely taking a breath.

And then I tasted raw terror. My escalating fears climaxed in the horror that someone, something was actually there, and what I saw in a few fleeting seconds sent shockwaves through every nerve in my body.

A face leaned out from behind the wall—a gray, nonhuman face. On its head sat an odd, sharply brimmed hat of the same color as the rest of the form. The brim dipped low over the upper portion of the gray creature's head and eyes, preventing a complete view, but in the seconds the intruder and I stood facing one another, barely five feet apart, I detected an expression on that gray, nameless face that I would swear was surprise. The creature who had somehow slipped beyond the locked doors appeared unprepared to find me standing there looking at it. And it was the unmistakable sentience detected within the eyes of that being as they stared into mine that made that gray alien face impossible to forget.

But by the count of three the face was gone. It did not dip back behind the wall. It seemed to simply disappear, vanish before my eyes.

From what I could remember of the following few minutes, I walked out into the kitchen only to find it empty. Upon inspecting the side doors, I found them locked and undisturbed. With no evidence to support what seemed to have just happened, I told myself that I must have imagined the sounds; I must have hallucinated the image, though nothing quite like that had ever happened to me before.

After checking on the sleeping children and surveying the other rooms, it became clear that there was no trespasser in the house. Everything was perfectly in order, and the night returned to its ordinary passage as I waited for the Pritchards to return.

"Oh, the *grays*," Mr. Dallek said. "They're very cold and scientific." That's what I heard over the phone when I got to the part about the gray alien face. It was proof enough for me that Gary Dallek was familiar with the subject of aliens. Now, with the door open to freely discuss my alien encounters, I explained to Mr. Dallek that I could remember seeing strange gray beings even as a child.

"What happened back then?" Mr. Dallek asked, and I proceeded to lay out the details of another night stamped into memory by a peculiar event.

That event also occurred in rural Wisconsin, in the house where I grew up, a five-bedroom farmhouse surrounded by hundreds of acres of fields, woodlands, and pasture—seemingly endless, open space. I was nurtured there in modest comfort with the special kind of homespun love and stability that is unique to large, rural families. Not only did I have both a mother and a father to care for me, but four older siblings were ever present to attend to my needs. Two more children would eventually complete my immediate family of nine.

As a child, I played on the farm's huge open stage, built from solid, guileless values, with nature, forever brilliant, forever changing, as the backdrop to my life. Everything about that world seemed perfect most of the time. There were, of course, family squabbles, sibling arguments, stress and tension now and then, but in view of what I've learned during my lifetime about other people's childhoods, even when mine was not absolutely perfect, it was still ideal and on the surface quite normal.

Everything appeared to be so normal and predictable during the first years of my life that I had little reason to question the sporadic occasions when something out of the ordinary did occur. Being resilient and hardy since birth, I usually adjusted to whatever life laid in front of me.

Still, there were those few exceptions, moments when bizarre things would happen that blatantly defied explanation, leaving me with the sense that the world, or at least my world, had temporarily fallen out of sync with time. With no labels by which to define such events, those bizarre experiences were simply added to the list of curiosities that slowly permeated my prosaic life.

The first of these unexplained experiences occurred while I was still very young. Though a lot of time divides then from now, my memory of that strange event has never dimmed. What I saw was truly unique, and because the bodies that appeared in the night behaved unlike any living organisms I had observed before, my young mind naturally grabbed hold of the images and my perceptions with such force that my memories were permanently anchored. It was truly a staggering experience for a three-year-old.

At that age, but only on occasions when the situation warranted such latitude, my parents would allow me to sleep with them. My bedroom was the only other sleeping room located on the first floor of the farmhouse and, according to my mother, sometimes I would wake up during the night and find my way down the hall to the master bedroom.

Only on one particular occasion, however, do I actually remember sharing my parents' bed. It was the night when I saw a procession of nonhuman lifeforms file into their room.

The beings approached without fanfare. They were silent and slow and curiously regimental. They moved as a collective body, displaying the kind of precision often demonstrated by soldiers during military formations. As they entered the bedroom, I noticed that they did not turn their heads to look at me. I also noted that their eyes never blinked. Like stiff, unsophisticated robots, they stared straight ahead, their long, skinny arms motionless at their sides.

As soon as I saw the beings approaching, I propped myself up on my elbows to look over at my mother. I fully expected to find her awake and watching the strange procession along with me, but her eyes were closed. She did not even stir. A quick study of my father's face told me that he, too, was still asleep.

A wave of confusion flowed through my mind at that moment; I couldn't understand how my parents could sleep through the activity that was taking place around them. Yet, I never tried to wake them up, maybe because I didn't have time, or maybe because the confusion I was feeling quickly dissipated when I looked up from the bed to see more of the strange beings file into the room.

I remember studying the beings mindfully, as any three-year-old would, looking for something familiar: a behavior or a facial feature that might help me identify the obscure beings. I was awed by the strangers' uniqueness. Though young and inexperienced, I knew that I was looking at an extraordinary form.

The creatures I observed that night had round, solid black eyes, hairless heads, and no noticeable noses or ears. Their faces appeared nearly flat, and their large, elongated heads sat atop necks that seemed too narrow, too thin to easily support such structures. Each being that came through the doorway looked exactly the same as the others—same height, same color, same features.

The grayish white beings were surrounded in a misty-white cloud that gave them a shimmering, almost translucent appearance. The cloud moved and expanded as if to accommodate the increasing number of bodies during their slow, forward march into my parents' bedroom. Because their entire bodies glowed, my three-year-old mind thought that the unknown entities looked like ghostly apparitions, though their shape and extreme characteristics did not resemble any phantom-like forms I had ever seen before.

Consumed in the strangeness of the moment, but buoyed by fascination, I quietly watched the beings as they continued to move into the room, first along the foot of the bed, then up the left side. More and more of the strange bodies entered until seven or eight of them stood as if in attention, arms perfectly still at their sides, while bordering and facing the bed.

The sight of the glowing, unearthly forms positioned around my sleeping parents and me was the oddest spectacle my young eyes had yet seen. I never forgot it. Nor did I ever forget the instructive thought that filled my mind during my last few seconds of consciousness, just before my memories of that incident end. It seemed as if a voice in my head was saying, "Lie back on the bed and everything will be all right. Go back to sleep and everything will be all right."

I responded by slipping underneath the blankets and obediently closing my eyes.

When I woke the next morning, I thought about the creatures, looking them over in my mind, while trying to come up with a reason for the experience. In spite of the ghostly glow emanating from the beings, they appeared very real. Nevertheless, at three years of age the only explanation I could fathom from my knowledge and understanding of the corporeal world was "It must have been a dream."

Yet, over the course of three decades, my mind never lost its grip on the experience or the inner sense that it was *not* just a dream. Then, when recalling the incident years later, after discovering that those grayish creatures were what people where describing as "aliens," that inner sense was again stirred up in my mind. I knew that it was impossible for thousands of other people, strangers to me, to have dreamed such peculiar creatures, too.

While explaining to Mr. Dallek what had taken place in my parents' bedroom, it occurred to me that I was talking to someone whose expertise was in helping people remember their past. That was not my problem. My memories were stuck in my mind like tiny slivers, clearly visible just under the surface, and gradually festering with time. Now they were causing pain and infecting my life with uncertainty. I didn't need someone to help me remember my past; I needed someone who could help me find a way to forget it.

"Looking back at these strange incidents," I said to Mr. Dallek, as we continued our phone conversation, "has convinced me that I've been involved with aliens for years. I suspect that I've been abducted, too. I've had dreams of being on spaceships, and other dreams—if they even were dreams—of seeing spaceships in the sky. I'm starting to remember all sorts of weird things that have happened to me during my life, and they all point to my involvement with these gray aliens.

"Remembering this stuff," I continued, "has started to impact my sleep. I've been waking up in the middle of the night in a panic. My heart's pounding. I'm terrified. The fear is so intense sometimes that I actually feel sick. And whenever it happens, whenever I wake up like that, which is usually around one or two o'clock in the morning, I'm too anxious to go back to sleep. So I lie in bed with the light on until dawn, until I feel that it's safe to close my eyes. I'm barely getting four solid hours of rest some nights," I added, "and I'm starting to feel like a wreck, both physically and emotionally."

Embracing the idea that the peculiar creatures crawling out of my past were the "aliens" thousands of other people had reported seeing gave my memories new meaning and recast my lifetime of unexplained events in the shape of an unsettling truth. I knew my memories were real. I knew I had seen alien forms step into the night, and now those forms represented a reality that had become too difficult to live with.

By the time I contacted Gary Dallek, a heavy, dark cloud was hanging over my life, a cloud of possibility that carried the question, "When will the aliens return?" That possibility was robbing me of sleep and stripping my nerves of their usual tolerance. Sudden loud noises now sent me leaping into the air, and if someone inadvertently surprised me from around a corner, I would let out a horrifying scream, often giving that poor, unsuspecting individual an unexpected start.

And, for the first time in my life, I was actually afraid to go to bed at night, afraid to be alone, but I lived alone. I was in my mid-thirties, yet experiencing the fears of a child, and not even my adult reasoning skills could assuage the dread that started to accompany the onset of night. Even such thoughts as "There's no logical reason to be afraid" or "The doors are locked, nothing can harm you" had no effect on the inner voice that kept my fears alive.

It seemed as if there was a little girl inside of me saying, "But there really are bogeymen," while a teenager could be heard yelling, "Run. Hide. Just run." And sometimes I could hear the adult woman inside my head screaming and screaming and screaming, though never understanding why.

Those screams did explain why I was now sitting in Gary Dallek's comfortable leather recliner and thinking that hypnosis was like a soft and beautiful dream, an escape from a reality that had become disturbingly real and unbearably painful. As Gary Dallek's voice continued to lead me away from the stress and anxiety of the present, I knew that by looking into the past there was a chance that I could make the bogeymen go away, and then I could reclaim my nights. At least that was what I thought I was doing; that was the goal of the hypnosis session.

But then I had no idea that my alien visitors had their own plans where I was concerned, and it never occurred to me that there might be some purpose to my encounters. Nor did I realize that it was time for me to learn the extraordinary secret of why aliens were a part of my life, and would be forever.

"All things, all thoughts, all feelings, all sensations will move you deeper here today. As you go deeper, you become aware. You breathe into the body and go deeper, now. Ten. Gently and easily moving deeper, now."

Only a few minutes had passed since I first closed my eyes to focus on the sound of Mr. Dallek's voice, but already my body felt heavy. The soft words flowing around me were working their soothing effect: acute physical and mental relaxation. I let that feeling travel down, down, deep into the core of my being. And with the suggestion now firmly planted in my brain, every subtle tap against my wrist took me deeper and deeper into a calm, floating, bodiless state of relaxation.

"Allow the word 'yes' to move into your mind, and as the word 'yes' moves into your mind, go deeper. Allow the energy of the word 'yes' to move all the way down to one of your fingers to be the 'yes' response signal. Allow that finger to lift and rise to let me know it means 'yes.'"

One of my fingers responded.

"And go deeper now as we allow the pointer finger on the right... as I touch your hand, go deeper.

"Allow the word 'no' to move into your mind to allow you to use the word 'no' to move all the way down to allow the finger to be a 'no' response signal. Allow that finger to lift and rise to mean 'no,' 'no,' and go deeper, now."

Again, a finger lifted.

"We will allow the pointer finger on the left to be that 'no' response signal—not having information available, not knowing, not having an answer, not having information available.

"Allow the subconscious mind to choose another response finger that means not knowing, not having an answer. Go deeper, now."

There was a pause, then Mr. Dallek continued, "We can allow the pinkie on the left to be that 'not knowing' response signal.

"I'd like you to allow the 'yes' finger to lift and drop and touch the chair. Each time it does so, you're going a thousand times deeper."

By now I could feel my mind, my awareness drifting away, farther and farther from the moment, from the room, until it was riding high on the back of every spoken word. I felt as though my body were drifting away too, gaining speed with each and every breath until some part of me separated from the physical reality around me. Both my mind and my body seemed to be lifting, rising, soaring into space like a swallow heading home after a long winter, with instinct leading the way.

"Continue moving yourself deeper until we can move to a level of working here today. And as you go deeper and deeper, each beat of your heart continues to move you a hundred times deeper, as the sound of my voice circulates and mixes with each and every out-breath. Always going deeper here today. Always moving deeper, going deeper, now.

"And we're going to move to a room of healing and knowledge. We're going to move down ten steps to profound relaxation. Each step will take you a thousand times deeper. At the number one step, the doorway will be open into this room of healing and knowledge. As we move from the tenth step, deeper now, down to the ninth and the eighth, deeper now, to the seventh, sixth, fifth, going deeper, go deeper now, down to the fourth, the third, the second, all the way down to one.

"As you step through the doorway into this room of healing and knowledge, the colors of this room are perfect healing colors. And this room is sealed and surrounded in an energy of healing light, as is your body sealed in light and protection as we work here today. As I seal my body in light and protection, I seal us in light."

CHAPTER 2

The Face of a Familiar Unknown

As you step into this room of healing and knowledge, in the very center of this room is a comfortable place, a special place for you to lie down. A place that supports your body perfectly in every way. So simply allow your mind to imagine or picture this comfortable place and allow yourself to go to that place, enhancing it with your ability to see, to feel, and get into these emotions. As you lie down, you go twice as deep. As you go deeper, you breathe into the body. As you breathe into the body, breathe out and go twice as deep, as each beat of your heart moves you a hundred times deeper."

Gary Dallek's suggestion to picture myself lying down on a comfortable place was a welcomed request. I seriously needed a long, long period of quiet relaxation to recover from months of physical, mental and emotional stress, and whether I rested in my mind or physically in the material world didn't really matter to me. I just needed to rest. I just wanted to close my eyes and know that I was safe, if even for a few minutes.

My childlike fears and the accompanying anxiety that had slowly, stealthily crept into my life had gradually destroyed any semblance my nights had to a normal sleeping routine. I was quickly learning that the cumulative effect of sleep deprivation was to wreak havoc with a person's physical health and their emotional stability.

But, in a way, I had only myself to blame for my present state of mind and body. I was the one who had instigated this whole mess by churning up the waters of the past, bringing to the surface a lifetime of cast-off perceptions and finding new meaning in old, unexplained memories.

It all began rather innocently, however. I was at a nearby video store scanning the rows, when I saw a video of the motion picture *Communion*. I pulled it off the shelf and read the back of the videotape's jacket. The movie was about Whitley Strieber's encounters with non-human lifeforms he called "the visitors."

I had noticed Strieber's book *Communion: A True Story* a few years earlier while browsing in an airport bookstore. The alien face on the cover, with its huge, dark eyes, aroused my curiosity just enough to inspire a brief inspection. But when I realized what the book was about, my interest quickly drained away. Reading about some guy's "true story" of encounters with alien beings was not how I wanted to spend three hours of flying time. Strieber must have been hallucinating, I readily concluded, or perhaps his imagination had gotten the best of him, and with that final thought I headed off toward the direction of my flight gate.

I was never one to argue the probability that nonhuman life forms existed elsewhere in the universe. As a teenager I had read three or four books about unidentified flying objects (UFOs) and on a regular basis had watched "Project Blue Book," a television program that aired in the 1970s and portrayed the efforts and findings of the U.S. Air Force UFO investigation unit known as Project Blue Book.

Based on information gleaned from these sources, I decided that at least the anomaly of UFOs had to be real. The sheer number of unidentified flying objects being reported around the world seemed proof enough of their existence, and there were too many unexplained sightings and uncanny similarities between the objects' descriptions to refute the fact that something unusual was flying around in our skies.

It seemed clear to me that if UFOs were actual aircraft, they had to come from somewhere. Why not outer space? No one on *this* planet was taking responsibility for them. My logic followed that someone had to be piloting those flying objects as well. Probably beings from outer space. But could human beings actually be coming into contact with life forms from some distant place in the cosmos? For some unknown reason that idea would only fit into my imagination, and it remained there throughout the 1980s.

I rented the movie *Communion* in early November 1990. Three years had gone by since Strieber's book, with the peculiar face on the cover, had hit the stands. I was living in Minneapolis, Minnesota, and working as an independent training consultant specializing in instructional design.

During most of that year, my time and attention were centered on the development of a series of corporate training materials that I was under contract to write, and a typical day meant long hours in my home office entertaining my computer. Watching a rented video was a frequent departure from my usual work routine, and it created an opportunity to stare at a different screen for a while, one that entertained me.

On that day in November, while standing in the neighborhood video store, it happened by chance that I selected the movie *Communion*, motivated only by my desire for an hour or two of mindless diversion.

But instead of providing light amusement as a brief escape from a day's focused concentrations, the movie weighed heavily on my mind. It continued to darken my mood even after I returned the video. During the days that followed, specific scenes from the movie would replay in my mind, scenes etched in memory by the flutter of fear they produced while I sat watching the movie alone.

I was not exactly sure why the spontaneous reruns kept playing over and over again, but the images that appeared in my mind forced me to admit that there was something oddly familiar about Strieber's experiences. He often felt compelled to search his house for some unknown "thing" that might be lurking in a closet or behind a door. I frequently searched areas in my residence, too, looking into closets, under the bed, and behind doors for something that might be hiding there. Though I rationalized that such behavior was unfounded, on certain occasions that before-going-to-bed ritual was a necessity before I could relax and fall asleep.

Then there were the nights when I would wake up in the early morning—typically between the hours of two and four—feeling uneasy, almost as if I had been spooked by something in my room. Even though I knew I was alone, there often remained a residual layer of perception suggesting that someone or something was actually in the house. Whenever that happened, I had to make a tour of all the rooms in order to get back to sleep. Every fiber of my being resisted climbing out of bed, still I would force myself to leave the security of my bedroom, and as quickly as possible turn on all the house lights while completing an inspection.

What was I looking for? I didn't have a clue, but during the early 1980s an image began to surface in my mind, an image of a skinny gray creature—not human—wearing a strange hat. I would see it looking up at me from a place near the floor, its bone-thin arms wrapped around its constricted, narrow body. I had no idea where that image was coming from, so I naturally explained it away as some weird design created by my imagination.

It all seemed so ridiculous, so absurd—the eccentric nocturnal behaviors and seemingly unprovoked fears—until the day I watched *Communion* and saw myself in Strieber's character trying damn hard to prove that there was nothing to be afraid of.

Other aspects of the movie also struck a familiar chord. Strieber was often overwhelmed by the unshakable sense that his dreams were not dreams but actual, perceived events. I knew that feeling associated with my own peculiar dreams. But while Strieber came to believe that the strange alien creatures in his bedroom were real, I was still assuming that the unearthly beings that occasionally appeared next to my bed were subconsciously manufactured dream figures.

The scenes from *Communion* that were playing back through my mind gradually faded away, except for one particular scene, and that scene did not surface until several weeks later. Actually, it was an image from the movie that had apparently made an impact on my psyche, because one day it just popped into my head. That image, though visible during the movie for less than five seconds, must have been recorded into memory, then buried, locked away until my mind was ready to look at it again.

The scene showed Strieber sitting on a chair next to his bed. It was early morning, and his wife was sleeping soundly only a few feet away. He whispered into the dim light, "Is that somebody there?" Switching to Strieber's point of view, the camera focused on an armoire positioned to the left of the door leading out of the room. Suddenly, from around that piece of furniture, a face appeared, a nonhuman, alien face, with strange dark eyes. Seconds later, it mysteriously disappeared from view.

It was the image of the alien's face that had covertly crept into my unconscious. When it slipped out from its hiding place to appear again in my mind, it deposited there a vague emotional weight. Visualizing that image made me extremely uncomfortable.

My insides would tighten up whenever I remembered the alien, especially how it looked as it slowly, cautiously leaned out from the shadows.

My immediate reaction was to ban the alien's face from my thoughts, hoping to get rid of it forever, and for a while, I was able to make the image go away.

During December 1990 and January 1991, my professional life demanded all of my mental energy, thereby thoroughly chasing away all memories of alien faces. But in February, my work responsibilities briefly changed when I finally completed the first draft of a training course I was writing. I knew it would be several days before revisions on that project would come back from my client, and with no new commitments keeping me at my computer keyboard, I decided to spend a few days with my cousin, Sheila Castleberg, and her family.

Sheila and I had known each other practically forever. First brought together as babies, we developed a deep and lasting friendship early in life. Our long history as cousins resulted in volumes of shared experience, enhanced by the fact that our interests followed in many of the same directions. One of those directions pointed toward the unknown.

As teenagers, Sheila had Tarot cards; I had a Ouija board. We both liked movies and books about ghosts, monsters, astrology, the occult, and UFOs. We even liked "the macabre," especially in the form of the old horror flicks. But we were not fanatical about any of our interests. We were just inquisitive kids with a taste for the unusual.

During childhood, through adolescence and for much of my adult life, Sheila was the only person with whom I felt comfortable discussing anything unusual that was occurring in my life. She knew my moods, my idiosyncrasies, my hopes, and my dreams. I trusted her with my life stories, and I always knew she would be open-minded when it came to discussing something extraordinary or merely something new. Sheila, however, was often one step ahead of me when it came to discovering what was new, which was again the case when I told her about the movie *Communion*.

"Sheila, I saw a video a few months ago that you'd probably like," I said to my cousin, as we settled into comfortable places within the quiet of her bedroom. With two adolescent boys in the house, we often had to disappear to one of the many rooms located on the second floor of the Castlebergs' stately, three-generation farmhouse. There we could talk for an hour or so and not be interrupted.

"Really? What was it?" she asked.

"It was called *Communion*, and it was about this guy named Whitley and his encounters with aliens." I then waited to hear her reaction.

Sheila rose up off her ankles from where she had been sitting cross-legged on the floor. "I've seen it and read the book, too," she responded casually, while pulling two pillows across the comforter covering the bed. "I have another book, *Transformation*, that was written by the same author."

From the upholstered chair and ottoman—my favorite place to lounge during our chats in the master bedroom—I watched my long-time friend slide the front of her body across the bed. She propped her elbows up with the pillows, then stretched her legs back toward the head of the bed.

Facing me again, only now from a more comfortable position, Sheila added, "If you want to read *Communion* or *Transformation*, or both books, I'll give you my copies. Remind me to look for them before you go back to the Twin Cities."

We spent the next hour exploring the concept of alien abduction and discussing Whitley Strieber's encounters as depicted in the movie. Sheila shared what she remembered from Strieber's book and told of similar cases she had read about in other books, mostly written by individuals researching the alien contact and abduction phenomena.

It was during that discussion with Sheila when I first became aware of how pervasive human encounters with aliens had become. People from around the world were reporting such incidents. That realization, as incredible as I thought it was, rumbled through my brain like thunder from a distant storm. Encounters...gray beings in the night...humans taken from their houses...spaceships...other dimensions...strange eyes.

Then, like dense, dark clouds building overhead, scenes from my own life began to take form. Images flashed across my mind: an alien face...odd ships in the sky...gray rooms with circular walls. As the images condensed on the walls of my consciousness, my memories began falling like rain.

Out of my mouth gushed stories of my own strange and puzzling experiences, stories seldom told but impossible to forget. Even Sheila, my trusted confidante, had never heard most of these stories before. I had thought that they bordered on the fringes of reality—I could hardly believe them myself. It had always been easier to dismiss them than to try to explain what had occurred.

Among the incidents I described to my cousin was the night I was babysitting at the Pritchards', the night the gray face peered out at me from around the corner. I explained how my memories from that evening would periodically drift through my thoughts, causing me to wonder how it was possible for a person like me—someone capable of distinguishing reality from fantasy—to manufacture all that took place during one unforgettable night.

I knew that the things I heard and saw in the Pritchards' home that night were perceived as conscious elements, each carrying the familiar and abundant properties ascribed to events in reality. And, had it not been for the sound of footsteps, I would never have concluded that someone had entered the house. With the doors locked and the windows undisturbed, that simply was not possible, nor was it likely that anyone would even attempt to break into a house in rural Wisconsin when someone was obviously home. Yet, my senses had perceived the noise, the footsteps, and the face.

I told Sheila that even though I had decided to label the gray face a hallucination, I never really believed that it was. There were too many unanswered questions undermining that assumption. For instance, if I had been hallucinating, why would I concoct a nonhuman face, and a gray one, at that? And why would my own imagination turn against me and design an event that would frighten me out of my wits?

While Sheila and I discussed these questions and explored the details I remembered from that strange night at the Pritchards', I was surprised to find that my memories—now more than twenty years old—still evoked the same emotions I had experienced as the peculiar events unfolded, including the heart-stopping horror I felt the moment I laid eyes on the gray face. And while Sheila pointed out the similarities between my experiences and those associated with alien abductions—unexplained lights, animal exhibiting unusual behaviors, the sudden appearance of strange gray beings—those old emotions twirled into an unsettling question: Could the creature that peered out at me from around the corner have been an alien?

I wasn't ready to answer that question. Aside from what Sheila had told me about the subject of alien abductions and what I had learned from watching *Communion*, I knew almost nothing about the phenomenon. But I wanted to know more, and so my quest began.

I returned to Minneapolis with Sheila's copies of *Communion* and *Transformation*, and during the days that followed I read almost constantly, searching for clues that might link me to the alien abduction phenomenon. The evidence I sought was definitely there: the dream-like encounters, the gaunt gray creatures, even Strieber's thoughts and emotions mirrored my own. I was astounded to learn that even some of the aliens' odd behavior that I had observed—walking in lockstep, for instance—were mentioned. It seemed doubtful that such bizarre similarities could be explained as mere coincidences, especially when the subjects being compared were not even of this earth.

After finishing Strieber's two books, I rented *Communion* once again, and while immersed in the experiences of another, more scenes from my own life sprang into view. The odd familiarity I experienced while watching the video the first time quickly matured into an overwhelming sense of association. As I recalled bits and pieces of the unexplained peculiarities that had occurred throughout my life, I felt as though I was discovering a secret part of myself that had long been forgotten.

Then it finally struck me: I suddenly understood why the image of the gray alien in the movie had continually crept back into view. That image reminded me of the face I had seen with my own eyes many years before, while standing in the Pritchards' living room. It was the face of a familiar unknown, burned long ago into memory, and now a face I wanted to forget.

CHAPTER 3

Exploring the Unexplained Past

WHAT STARTED OUT AS a casual conversation between Sheila Castleberg and me had ended in an unsettling discovery: my involvement in the alien abduction phenomenon, or at least the possibility of involvement. At that specific point in time, I still viewed the concept of human interaction with aliens as something highly unusual and truly bizarre. I was not comfortable accepting the idea that I had experienced a face-to-face encounter with a nonhuman being. Besides, I wondered, what would an alien life form want with me?

That question, along with a sea of other issues, bounced around in my head during the weeks that followed my conversation with Sheila, and before long another flood of old memories spilled into view. This time, a steady stream of peculiar scenes flowed out across my mind, suggesting that my unconscious had finally lifted the floodgate, releasing a current of curiosities that had been conveniently left in the past.

I remembered events from my childhood, events I had assumed were dreams. I remembered floating down, down, down during the night in a tube of blackness, waiting to be returned to my crib. I remembered standing at the top of the second-floor stairway with strangers who arrived during the night, then floating down the stairs instead of walking, a sensation I experienced many times. I remembered waking up during the night, only to realize that I was not in my bed, but alone in the woods near my house—a terrifying moment that became a recurring nightmare.

It also seemed that some earlier memories had only been the abbreviated view, and that more detailed recollections were simply waiting around the bend of time to be consciously acknowledged, then carefully sorted through. For instance, I started seeing the image of a small alien craft on the lawn outside the Pritchards' home, the curious detail of the farm's windmill rising up behind the craft still clear within my view. I was positioned between the windmill and the house, and at some point I must have turned around because I could see the Pritchards' two children. They were standing at the end of the sidewalk, just beyond the side entrance to the house, and they were dressed in their pajamas. The youngest was clutching a blanket, and both children were rubbing their eyes as if just coming out of sleep.

Such scenes forced another avalanche of questions: If aliens are real, who are these creatures? Where do they come from? Why are they taking humans out of their homes during the night? What do they want from us? And again I would ask, Why would I be involved in their schemes? Because I was not ready to accept my personal involvement with aliens, I often posed yet another, though less-threatening, question: Was there another explanation for the strange incidents that had dotted my life?

The answers came, but only after I traveled down a long, long road of inquiry.

I continued to research the alien abduction phenomenon, reading books with telling titles such as *Intruders* and *Encounters*. After scouring the stories and personal accounts contained within only a small sampling of the available UFO and alien abduction literature, I quickly realized that the shimmering visitors who had advanced into my parents' bedroom during a dark and silent hour, and who perhaps were the strangers vaguely remembered from childhood, were of a breed whose calling card had indeed been left with others. That calling card, however, was often completely buried in the minds of the humans who were visited, and a long period of time typically ensued before an abductee's memories eventually surfaced. Even then, those memories often took the form of fragmented images, vague impressions and diffused fear.

Many of the personal accounts reported as alien abductions, and sworn as true by the individuals who had witnessed them, were filled with very specific details. The descriptive narratives of what these men and women had experienced while in a realm they had never set foot in before reminded me of my own recollections:

> ...he has a neck, but it's small, like the rest of him. Skinny. His chin is really pointy, too. I don't see any ears, although there's something there. There's a slit where his mouth should be, but it's not open...[1]

> ...he's got a very large hairless head, gray skin, big blackish-brown eyes—big eyes—sort of, sort of slanted; tiny holes in the, in the nose and sort of a slit in the mouth part. And he had a very large head. It goes down very narrow at the chin.[2]

Because such descriptions offered another glimpse of the grayish white beings I first encountered in my parents' bedroom, I had no choice but to admit that my visitors on that evening looked remarkably similar to the so-called aliens who had entered the homes of individuals reporting alien abductions.

Those individuals were also not any different from me, just ordinary people with regular lives. They were educated, responsible citizens, many were professionals. Some had first seen the cloudy-white beings when they were children, while others had encountered them later in life. Yet all had been visited by peculiar beings reminiscent of my childhood visitors.

Everything I had learned up to that point from the UFO and alien abduction literature suggested that nonhuman sentient life forms were indeed interacting with thousands of people from all parts of the globe. The similarities among the accounts presented in the literature were astounding.

Still, I searched my mind for other possible explanations of why so many people might be experiencing similar encounters with the unknown. Pondering that question led me to conclude that it was highly unlikely that people were inventing their stories or that aliens were merely archetypal figures appearing in dreams. The creatures' alien form, as compared to the body of a human, made it difficult to imagine that any two people could conjure up the same image. Even less likely was the chance that the thousands of men and women recalling alien encounters, mostly strangers to one another, would dream the same design. And, within every new book I read on the subject of alien abduction, I discovered more unique parallels between my own recollections and the characterizations of aliens provided by people who were totally unknown to me:

> There's at least three or four....Humanoid appearance. Kind of cloudy white color....Their features are flatter and less prominent than the human face.[3]

> I was three (or so)....Little "white" men...came into my room. They looked like "Casper, the friendly ghost" to me. There were five or six of them....They spoke without voices—I heard them in my head. They tried to get me out of my bed. I was afraid, but I knew that my daddy and mommy would not help me.[4]

In questioning the source and validity of my own experiences, I would have considered it possible that film and literary encounters with aliens had manifested into images later reproduced in my dreams, that is, if I had been in my teens or twenties when I first saw the strange creatures. But that explanation fell short in my situation because my initial encounter with aliens occurred when I was just a little girl. My first experience with these odd-looking life forms was recorded in memory when I was at an age when any exposure to the media would have been extremely limited.

Visualizing myself as that three-year-old child, sitting on the bed between my sleeping parents, forced me to wonder what else might have happened to me at the hands of aliens, especially in view of my changing perspective around the events I remembered from that strange night. It was impossible not to wonder, not to speculate, because others who had witnessed the same or similar alien beings often reported bizarre and shocking experiences at the hands of their alien intruders:

> *I only see two of them. [Pause] They help me over to a table. I lie down....Small people. Shaped like people. Little. Round heads...pretty round. Slim-featured....They're just, they're examining me, I guess. I don't know what they're doing. They've got all my clothes off. They're looking at me all over. Ears, eyes, mouth, they look my body all over.*[5]

> *The beings then started to examine and probe my body with long thin metal instruments scanning over my body and some were inserted vaginally and rectally. The only memory I have after that is being back in bed...*[6]

Invasive procedures similar to medical exams were frequently reported by abductees. Knowing this made it even more difficult to accept the reality of the alien abduction phenomenon, especially my involvement in it. With each new account that I read depicting scenes of alien experimentation on humans, my level of anxiety heightened, until a feeling close to fear sat like a ticking bomb within my psyche, waiting to explode into a shower of dread and indignation.

When I searched through my recollections from the night the luminous beings entered my parents' bedroom, I stepped lightly across the floor of my psyche, delicately looking for evidence that would answer the question that now plagued my mind: Had I been removed from my parents' bedroom and taken to some place where aliens would have experimented on me?

I could not remember physically leaving the bed while the alien creatures were in sight, but sitting among my memories was a lone image that suggested that I had. Sometime during the encounter I had viewed the aliens from a location other than the bed. What I had seen as a little girl was a view of the aliens' feet. I specifically remember scrutinizing that feature because the feet were definitely out of the ordinary. There were no ankles at the ends of the aliens' bone-thin legs, only a long, flat toe-less protrusion that extended at a ninety-degree angle from the lower leg, and whatever covered their bodies also appeared to extend down over their feet.

The mystery surrounding that image evolved out of the realization that it would have been impossible for me to see the aliens' feet from my position on the bed. Yet the image, firmly shaped by the focused perceptions of a curious child, had clearly been perceived and recorded in my mind. I was pressed to believe that during the night I had indeed left my place on the bed and accompanied my eccentric bedside visitors to some unknown place.

The fact that I did not remember leaving with the shimmering beings did not guarantee that such an event had never happened. It was generally believed among alien abduction researchers that aliens were capable of inducing some form of amnesia to mask certain memories from the minds of their human targets. Supporting this theory were the abductees' own reports. Many individuals were able to recall that their alien captors had specifically told them—telepathically—that they would not remember what took place or recall any communications that transpired during their encounters.

Some abductees were so angry after being taken out of their homes or their cars against their wishes and subjected to humiliating and distressing procedures that they consciously countered the aliens' telepathic suggestions with thoughts such as, "I *will* remember everything" and "I *won't* let them make me forget what happened." Others had even tried to bring back material evidence to validate their encounters, but the aliens always prevented such attempts.

Despite the aliens' efforts to erase their presence from people's minds, in many contact and abduction cases an emotional residue or a fragmented image still remained after the abduction experience. It was often these leftover feelings and perceptions that, over time, brought the experience back into the abductee's mind.

Hypnosis was sometimes used to explore these fragmented images and vague perceptions. In her book *Encounters*, Dr. Edith Fiore used hypnosis as a tool to help a woman named Sandi recall additional events that were part of a strange incident she remembered from her past.

Prior to hypnosis, Sandi could remember that on the night of the incident she had been watching television when she noticed a bright light through a nearby window. As she stared at the light, the television picture "turned to black and white snow." Sandi remembered feeling immobilized, yet didn't recall how much time had elapsed before the television screen returned to normal and she was able to move her arms and legs again.

During the hypnosis session, Sandi recounted what had happened during the time she was immobilized. She described being taken aboard a UFO and subjected to a series of bizarre procedures at the hands of alien creatures:

> *They're turning my head to look at the back of my neck. My neck doesn't go that way.... When they touched me, they were cold. I didn't like it, but they were gentle. I remember telling them, "No! No, don't you do that to me! Don't you do that to me!" [Cries] And they were telling me that it would be okay.*

*They were trying to settle me down. And I didn't want them
doing that to me. They were going to put something up my rectum, and I...[Crying hard]...didn't want them to do that to me.*[7]

The alien encounter that Sandi recalled with the help of hypnosis once again depicted a scene resembling a medical examina-
tion. Sandi's "exam" involved a probe or a needle that she thought
was briefly inserted into her rectum. In other abduction accounts,
women reported that the aliens performed procedures to remove
ova from their bodies. Men, on the other hand, often recalled that
the strange beings placed devices over their genitals, presumably
for the purpose of obtaining sperm samples.

Individuals researching the abduction phenomenon often speculated that aliens might merely be conducting physical examina-
tions on humans and collecting specimen samples just as human
scientists do when studying an unknown life form. Some
researchers believed that in addition to human anatomy, aliens
also had a specific interest in human genetics, hence the need to
collect eggs and sperm from their subjects. It also had been suggested that aliens were carrying out breeding programs involving
genetic alterations, a concept supported by a number of
abductees who reported seeing children during their encounters
who looked like a cross, or hybrid, between humans and aliens.

A majority of abductees were also remembering, either with
the aid of hypnosis or through self-examination of childhood
memories, that alien encounters had been occurring throughout
their lifetimes. In many cases, the encounters were still happening, leading one to suspect that the aliens' research design was
perhaps longitudinal, especially since a large number of adult
abductees were aware that their children were now involved in
the aliens' surreptitious activities.

Before conducting my own research into the alien abduction
phenomenon, stories like Sandi's would have been impossible to
accept as anything but dreams, fantasies, or hallucinations. I
might have even proposed that the bizarre tales of abduction

retold while under hypnosis were fashioned out of the hypnosis experience itself, with the images and activities of aliens possibly produced in a subject's mind by an active imagination. But after reading dozens of personal accounts from a variety of sources and identifying scores of similarities between the various tales of close encounters, a definite pattern began to emerge, a pattern too tightly woven to be anything but the abductees' truth: strange lights; alien visitors; being physically taken or curiously lifted up into some craft or a room; telepathic conversations; outlandish procedures, often interpreted as clinical exams; then, being returned, either physically transported or floated through the air to the abductee's original location.

From my readings about the alien abduction phenomenon, I also learned that a distinguishing earmark to a possible abduction experience was "missing time"—the apparent loss of memory within a specific time interval.

Budd Hopkins' book, *Missing Time*, for example, describes several missing-time cases, each highlighting the story of an individual who, through the aid of hypnosis, discovered that his or her lost minutes or hours were spent in the company of alien beings.

Episodes of missing time are discussed in other books as well. In *The Omega Project*, Kenneth Ring, Ph.D., points out that periods of missing time are commonly reported in association with UFO sightings, giving this example:

> *...a forty-five-year-old attorney stated that following his seeing a fearful light in the sky (which he is now convinced was a UFO) while driving in his automobile, he found that he had arrived at his destination inexplicably two to two-and-a-half hours late. "I couldn't account for the missing time," he comments.* [8]

"At least I don't have any periods of missing time associated with my bizarre encounters," I once told a close friend, expressing relief in holding to that assumption. The characteristic of missing time appeared to be absent from my remembered past. But eventually even that feature became linked with my memories of strange, unexplained life events. I discovered a possible missing-time episode when my older brother John challenged my recollection of a particular incident that had occurred years earlier. The conflict between our memories sent me searching through my mental files for the details of that event.

Like many of the unexplained events in my past, this happened near my parents' farm in Wisconsin. It occurred during a weekend when I was visiting my family, as I was attending college in Minnesota and no longer living at home. I had driven into the nearby village to meet a friend for a couple of drinks and to catch up on her news. But later that night, while on my way back to the farm, I came up against a terrifying situation.

It was several minutes before midnight when I left the bar where my friend and I had met. By the time I left the lighted streets of the village and headed north into the night, it was even closer to the midnight hour. Ten minutes ticked away before I turned off the main highway and onto the gravel road that provided passage through the rolling wooded countryside and up to the hilltop where a number of dairy farms, including my family's operation, could be found scattered across the open land. Thirty more seconds passed before the car's steering wheel started to pull forcefully to the right. That action brought the vehicle quickly onto the shoulder of the road, where I stopped the car.

I climbed out to inspect the right front tire and, as I'd guessed, found it completely deflated. Looking down at the flattened rubber, I knew it would be impossible to drive the car any farther without damaging the wheel. Since it was doubtful that another driver would come along to offer me a ride, my only alternative was to walk home, a distance not much more than a mile.

I slid back into the driver's seat to contemplate my situation. I was sitting in the middle of a coulee flanked by a thick cover of trees. In order to get home, I would have to walk through the woods and up the hill. By day, the coulee road was a peaceful, natural setting, but by night...well, I had never walked on that road at night before, nor had I walked anywhere at night before without someone else at my side.

I told myself that everything would be fine. After all, I thought, I just had to walk a mile. Still, I warily searched the shadowy regions beyond the reach of the car's headlights before punching in the light button that made the view ahead turn black.

I waited in the car for a few seconds, allowing my eyes to adjust to the darkness. Then I remembered how much I hated being in the dark and being alone in the woods at the night.

My fear of the dark, the woods, the night, however, never made any sense to me; it seemed uncharacteristic of my nature and my experiences as a child growing up in the country. I loved the outdoors and viewed it as nature's fantasyland, a place where double rainbows could be seen stretching across the sky, a place where sparkling icicle forests magically appeared after a freezing rain. The outdoors had always been an elaborate playground that by design begged to be explored, promising spectacular discoveries for those who were willing to wander through it, with ears and eyes ready, of course.

I had spent thousands of hours exploring the river, woods, fields, and roadways within a five-mile radius from my family's farm. In fact, many of those hours were spent walking, jogging, riding a bike, or driving a car up and down the very road where my car sat with a flat tire. I had even hiked and hunted in the woods that bordered that road, and in all the time I spent roaming around in those woods, never had I seen or heard anything that warranted caution or fear. That expanse of nature was simply a home to deer, raccoon, fox, squirrels, pheasants, partridge, and other harmless creatures—with the exception of an occasional rattlesnake.

Besides being well aware of the spaces around the farm, I learned well from my rural environment of nature's varying conditions. I had witnessed the birth of calves, kittens, pigs, and pups, and been present at their final moments in death. I had labored in fields, chicken coops, cow yards, pig pens, and barns, sweating and freezing in enough rain, dirt, dust, mud, and snow to understand that the elements pay no favors to the unprepared. And I had been stepped on by cows, laid on by horses, stung by electric fences, thrown off wagons, and tipped out of trees. By the time I left the farm to go to college, I had learned much by way of nature. As a result, I was not easily unnerved or readily intimidated by it, and I was definitely not squeamish to the sights of life and death.

But in view of the beautiful and secure surroundings I grew up in, and in spite of my respect for and appreciation of its limits where living creatures were concerned, I still developed a particular phobia during my years on the farm. There was something that I truly feared. I feared it more than anything else in the world, and I discovered that it could fill me with dread and take me from sound to insane in an instant.

The thing I mysteriously learned to fear most was the dark, especially the dark caused by night, and specifically the kind of dark that permeated still and gentle country nights. If someone had made me choose between walking alone through a crime-ridden neighborhood at three o'clock in the morning or taking a quiet stroll by myself down a lone country road at that same hour, I would have chosen the threatening neighborhood without batting an eye. As long as I could remember, I had been afraid of being in the dark while in the country at night.

When my tire went flat on that stretch of country road, it was several minutes past midnight. There I was in the middle of the dark, in the middle of the woods, in the middle of the night. The situation reminded me of the recurring nightmare I remembered from my childhood—the dream in which I would wake up during the night and discover that I was no longer in my bed, but standing in a wooded area encircled by towering trees. That memory slid down tight against my present predicament, and I could see that I was about to experience nothing less than my worst night-mare coming true.

I remained in the car for another thirty seconds, long enough to wish that I had stayed in town for at least one more drink. In view of what I was about to do, I thought that the extra alcohol would have bolstered my courage or at least numbed my senses to a degree.

I then questioned whether or not I should take the flashlight from the glove compartment to light my way up the hill, but decided against it. I concluded that a light would only draw attention to my presence on the road, and I wanted to be as inconspic-uous as possible.

Exactly what I wanted to hide from was never clear to me—but, of course, I wasn't thinking clearly about anything anymore. I was simply reacting to the situation at hand, and my logic, normally available to guide my emotions, never made it through the fear that smothered my rational mind.

As soon as I left the security of the car, a dense wave of anxiety spread through me. Within seconds of stepping out into the night, the murky darkness closed in and reduced me to a mad, hysterical woman. I had barely taken ten steps from the car before I panicked.

I was sensing that something threatening was very near and about to seize me. My fate seemed evident: I was going to die. During the minutes I spent on that dark country road, surrounded by the shadows of night, a part of me suddenly relinquished my hold on life. I simply gave up; I surrendered. I was ready to hand over my soul without even a fight, believing that there was noth-ing I could do to protect myself.

But I started to run up the hill anyway, though my mind was drowning in terror, and all the while I prayed for the end to come quickly.

In all my days, at least up to that point in time, I had never known myself to be that afraid, that out of control. Each running stride took me one step closer to pain, one step closer to certain doom, and one step closer to the form that began to take shape on the road ahead. Something or someone appeared to be standing a few yards ahead of me. I slowed to a walk, straining my eyes to make out its features. Bound by fear, confusion, and the sense of inevitability, I continued to walk toward it, allowing my life essence to slowly slip away.

When I go back in time to that moment, exploring the details in my mind, I can't remember what happened to the form on the road. My next memory is of running again, running until exhaustion forced me to walk. If I'd had a weak heart, I'm sure I would have actually died there on the road, not at the hands of anything lurking in the night, but from fear alone. My adrenaline pumped out so fast that by the time I reached the top of the hill and cleared the woods I felt diluted, nauseated. I think I would have fainted if not for the soothing vista that opened up before my eyes.

A star-filled sky cast its dim light down around me and illuminated the familiar farms and broad stretches of corn and hay that brought me back to a place in reality. That welcomed sight reassured me that I would safely reach my home, and I gradually calmed down enough to grab hold of my emotions and to tell myself that I was going to be all right.

Five minutes later, I was walking through the back door of my parents' house.

Once inside, I decided to wake my older brother and ask his advice on whether I should leave the car until morning or change the tire yet that night. Being concerned about the hour and aware that John would probably not appreciate having his sleep disturbed, I estimated the time between 12:30 and 12:45 a.m.

"John, it's Janet," I said, knocking on his door. I then waited for a response. When it came, I explained the situation.

Nearly a decade would pass before my memories of what took place one summer night on the coulee road would ever come

back into question. I had always viewed the nightmarish experience as testimony to what fear can do to a rational mind, particularly when frightening events resemble the fears of childhood.
That perspective changed, however, when a playful conversation
prompted me to take another look.

My brother and I were having a discussion one day about past
good deeds and who owed what to whom. John reminded me that
he had once gotten up in the middle of the night to change a flat
tire for me. I reminded him that it was not much later than 12:30
when I roused him from his slumber. "It was later than that," he
said. "It was at least 1:30 or 2:00 in the morning."

Remembering the terror I experienced that night, and being
fully aware that my personal history included events mirroring
alien abduction episodes, I wondered if something else had taken
place during my frantic flight up the coulee road. Had I actually
lost an hour of time, maybe more? And what had initiated that
thundering rise of hysterical fear? Were hidden memories pro-
voking the terror that exploded in my mind whenever I found
myself outside at night and alone?

The fear and terror had been a part of my life since childhood.
By the time I had reached an age when it was prudent for my
parents to leave me at home by myself, my fear of the dark and
the night was already well established. Fortunately, being left
alone was not a frequent experience. Growing up in a large family prevented that situation from developing very often. But, in
the few cases when I was left alone within the confines of our
five-bedroom farmhouse, I always felt extremely anxious and vulnerable. My senses would stand on guard, and though my intellect told me it was unnecessary, I took every precaution to
protect myself against intruders. Sometimes, I would even bring
our dog, who was not allowed in the house, into the entryway as
a line of defense.

Another precautionary measure that I performed when left alone at night took on the character of a ritual. My parents never used to lock the back door of the house when they went away, not even when the entire family left the farm on Sunday to go to church, or when visiting friends or relatives, or during family shopping trips to distant cities. Crime in the area was nearly nonexistent; there was little threat of vandalism, burglary, or theft. Yet, when I was left alone in the house at night, locking the back door was the first thing I would do once my family drove out of sight.

After securing both the front and back doors, I would check the windows, draw down the shades, close all the curtains, and turn on as many lights as I needed in order to feel safe. I would then usually watch television to pass the time. Later, when I would see car lights turn into the driveway and assure myself that it was my family's car, I would run to unlock the back door, then run back into the living room.

It was not that my parents would have been opposed to having the door locked while they were gone; I just didn't want to admit that I was scared to death whenever I was alone in the house at night. I knew, too, that if I was questioned about my behavior, I would not have been able to explain my fears. They seemed so irrational, so absurd, even to me. I thought they embodied some form of emotional baggage carried over from my childhood, baggage that I should have thrown away a long time before.

Still, in spite of my varied efforts to quell my fears through rationalization, logic, and locked doors, I never managed to placate my guarded inner mind. My fears were extremely difficult to put down.

What never occurred to me as a young girl, or later as a teenager, was the possibility that my fears might be founded on genuine experience. If I was being abducted by aliens or encountering strange beings at night from time to time, I would have had great cause to feel threatened. Somewhere deep inside my mind I would have known that there really were creatures that roamed the night. Such an awareness would have warranted my guarded behavior; it would have motivated my protective instincts to rally on behalf of my own defenses whenever I was left alone. And if my unconscious mind knew more than it was willing to share with its conscious counterpart, the same instincts that sprang forth to protect my physical well-being would have continued to direct whatever mental devices it had been using to shield me from shocking realities that I was too young to easily accept.

The barrage of strange images that surfaced while I explored my possible association with aliens made me think that my childhood fears might not have been childish at all. They could have been rooted in repressed memories, potent memories, emotionally charged, some of which seemed to be coming out of hiding at last. But there were other memories too, memories sitting in my conscious awareness where they had been for many years. I never thought of them as reasons to fear the dark, the night, and being alone because they were labeled as weird dreams and unexplained events from my past.

These memories were available through recall, and included remnants as well as entire scenes from a lifetime of strange and perplexing events. They were forged into memory by bold, unmistakable images and perceptions too forceful and enduring to forget. Some of these memories would occasionally amble through my mind, seeking explanation in order and reason, but always without success. As a result, they remained labeled as curiosities.

But now, within the context of the alien abduction phenomenon, my bewildering dreams and life stories all made perfect sense. It amazed me how neatly they suddenly fell into place under the theme of "close encounters." I was also continually shocked to find aspects of my own experiences in the personal accounts of alien contactees and abductees:

The next thing I knew, I was sitting in a small sort of depression in the woods. It was quite dark, and frozen creeper was pressing tightly around me....Across the depression to my left there was a small individual whom I could see only out of the corner of my eye. This person was wearing a gray-tan body suit and sitting on the ground with knees drawn up and hands clasped around them. There were two dark eyeholes and a round mouth hole. I had the impression of a face mask.[9]

I'm in a forested area at night, a dark night. And I'm meeting some unearthly looking beings. Rounded heads and generally humanoid, but definitely not human. They have smaller, shorter bodies than an adult human and they're very lightweight....I didn't want to look at them close up, to see what they looked like.[10]

My childhood "dreams" held snatches of nightmarish episodes of waking up in the night, only to discover that I was standing alone in the middle of the woods. My perceptions during those incidents seized a few vague impressions that surprisingly managed to develop into complete thoughts in the midst of a mind heading toward hysterics. Although I was surrounded by darkness and could only discern brush and the foliage from nearby trees, I was always aware of my general location: Somehow I knew I was near my family's farm. I distinctly recall thinking that if I could only find my way out of the woods, I would be able to determine the direction of the farm and eventually find my way home.

What was even more disturbing than waking up in the middle of the night and discovering that I was no longer in my bed was knowing that the event would probably happen again. I experienced that nightmare at least four times before reaching my tenth birthday, and at some point thereafter I designated the event "my recurring bad dream."

The nightmare reoccurred so frequently during my youth that eventually I became conditioned to anticipate the dream's ending. Whenever I woke up and found myself standing in the

woods, I would override my fear by reminding myself that ulti-
mately I would wake up in the same, safe surroundings from
whence I came—back home and in my bed. That thought, however, provided little comfort upon awakening the next morning,
because the memory of being deposited in the middle of a dank
and eerie woodland remained highly intense.

The emotional impact of that erratic nightmare was further
strengthened by what I perceived in the woods. There was something very real about what I saw: the shadows and outlines of
trees cast in the dim light extending down from the night sky.
There was something very real about what I heard: the wind as it
weaved through the low vegetation and the nocturnal chatter of a
million insects. Upon waking in the morning, I was always left
with the cryptic feeling that I really had been deposited in the
middle of the woods during the night. That feeling, that suspicion,
grew stronger with each new occurrence until one morning I
actually checked my feet, my pajamas, under the blankets, and
the area next to the bed for debris from the woodland floor. I
found nothing. There was never any proof of where I might have
been during the night, and so the "dream" remained an enigma.

Another odd "dream," remembered from my late twenties or
early thirties, was also recast in memory while reading an abduction account. In that dream, I was walking along the side of a
knoll in the company of a small group of strangers. We traveled in
single file, following a trail that led upward toward the top of the
hill. An inch or two of snow covered the ground, and during the
dream it occurred to me that I was not exactly dressed for the
conditions, though I don't recall ever being cold.

As we trekked diagonally across the slope, my thoughts conveyed the normal curiosity that waking suddenly in a new situation would naturally evoke: I wondered what I was doing there,
where we were going, and what was at the top of the snow-covered mound. Looking in that direction, there was nothing else to
see. Beyond the terrain was only the backdrop of an overcast sky.
Still, the hilltop seemed to be our destination.

When we reached the top of the hill, everyone gathered around what looked like a hole in the ground. The opening was barely four feet in diameter. Although no words were spoken, I knew that I was supposed to go down into the hole. Looking over the edge into what I could then see was a dimly illuminated shaft, I wondered how that would be possible. There did not appear to be any steps or rungs or ledges to permit me to climb down, and the shaft went straight down for at least thirty or forty feet.

But before I had a chance to protest, I was already moving, floating, over the edge of the opening. My body seemed to be under someone else's control. As I entered the shaft, my mind was still questioning how I would crawl down the steep, rock-solid sides. That uncertainty triggered a sudden rush of anxiety, and then I completely lost consciousness.

The next thing I remembered was being at the bottom of the shaft and perceiving a totally unexpected sensation. A multitude of hands were supporting the weight of my disabled body. I felt them under my head, shoulders, back, hips, legs, and arms. Unable to move my major muscles, I spent the time mentally recording the sensation of being passed headfirst through the air.

It was a queer tactile experience, one I had never been subjected to before, certainly not as an adult, anyway. Yet, it was not an unpleasant experience. Whoever was moving me, handing off my body to different sets of open palms, did not seem to be in any rush. Their actions were slow, almost cautious, and their fingers, gentle, whenever I felt them carefully wrap around the curved portions of my horizontal frame. In fact, the individuals supporting me seemed to be taking great care in their effort. I even extracted from the moment a feeling of safety. Not only was I literally in other people's hands, but I felt as if I was in "good hands."

While reflecting on the odd "dream" the next morning, I also remembered that I had been in a small room that seemed like a receiving area. There was an open stairway leading down from another level, and the curves that defined the rounded shape of

the structure suggested that the stairway led up and out to the surface of whatever I was in. There were various items displayed in
the space around me, and many details of the structure were also
visible during the "dream," but my memory of those aspects grew
vague and cloudy by morning.

The collective strangeness of that peculiar episode came rushing back into my mind when I read the following passage in Whitley Strieber's *Communion*:

> *My memories of movement from place to place are the
> hardest to recall because it was then that I felt the most help-
> less. My fear would rise when they touched me. Their hands
> were soft, even soothing, but there were so many of them that
> it felt a little as if I were being passed along by rows of insects.
> It was very distressing.* [11]

I had not thought of my experience in exactly the same context
as "being passed along by rows of insects." Yet having rows of
hands touching your body at the same time is an unsettling sensation. I could easily relate to Strieber's reference.

Realizing that I could relate to other abduction scenarios
described in the UFO and alien abduction literature made it
increasingly apparent to me that my remembered dream life was
rife with events that fit perfectly into the alien abduction phenomenon. For instance, an account from *Secret Life*, by David M.
Jacobs, Ph.D., reminded me of a strange flight I once took:

> *...we went out the window....We're going straight up. I
> looked down and I saw the trees and everything on my street,
> and it makes me feel kind of scared because I don't really like
> heights....I know that we're going to some place.* [12]

Bizarre descriptions of floating through windows, which were
either closed or open, and traveling unaided through the air were
typical among the accounts retold as alien abductions. Though
highly peculiar in nature, my perceptions had recorded many

similar experiences—experiences that, in the context of alien encounters, could be viewed as real events merely masquerading as dreams.

One such encounter occurred when I was eighteen or nineteen years old, while I was at my parents' farm in Wisconsin for a weekend visit. During the night, I suddenly found myself sitting in a small aircraft, and though my mood was calm and passive, my senses were quick to absorb all that my strange surroundings offered.

The first thing I noticed was a dark-haired man sitting near the front of the craft. He was only an arm's reach away and wearing a black top that fit close to his body, akin to a knit turtleneck. I never heard him speak, but the serious manner in which he directed his attention out the broad windshield and then back to the console in front of him led me to believe that he was controlling the aircraft, though I didn't see anything on or around the console that resembled a steering device. It also appeared that the man and I were the only occupants in the cabin, but I don't remember ever turning around to look behind me.

From where I was sitting, I could easily see out the windshield and into the clear night sky. My perceptions told me that the craft was slowly moving through the air, less than a hundred feet above the ground. A road, sections of fields, and a wooded area were all within my field of vision.

The terrain below and in front of the craft was brightly illuminated. The cabin, on the other hand, was dimly lit, which created an obvious contrast between the visibility inside and outside the craft. In spite of the reduced lighting within the cabin's interior, I had no problem scrutinizing its aspects. The width of the cabin was not much more than six feet across, and space inside the craft was limited. Even though I was seated, there was little headroom, and I experienced the physical sensation of being cramped.

"Gee, did I have a weird dream last night!" I said, mentioning my nocturnal trip to someone in my family at the breakfast table. "I was flying over the farm in some type of airplane." That experience seemed weird to me for a couple of reasons. First, I wondered how I could create such a vivid flying experience in a dream when I had never been in an airplane before; my first airplane ride did not occur until I was twenty-one years old. I was amazed at how well my dreaming mind had captured what I could only guess to be the physical sensations of moving through the air while in some sort of aircraft. The second reason the dream seemed odd was that I remembered seeing the perfect aerial representation of several familiar landmarks.

While looking out the windshield from inside the craft, I immediately recognized a particular stretch of gravel, as well as the bordering woods and the fields up ahead and to the right. The aircraft was heading east, flying above a road that dropped down over a small hill toward an intersection of country roads referred to as "the Four Corners." Even the yellow and black directional sign that cautioned drivers of the winding road ahead was in view. While peering out a window located on the right side of the craft, I could see the distant outline of my parents' house and the farm buildings.

Everything that I observed during the night—the intersection of gravel roads, the fields, the woods, and the farm site—clearly indicated my location. But the view was unique, because I had never seen it from an aerial perspective before.

Another remarkable view I remembered from that "dream" added to the episode's incredulity. At some point in time, either before I was in the tiny aircraft or after, I looked down from a height of about sixty or seventy feet, and my entire view was filled with trees. I observed the treetops while floating over them, moving in a forward direction and under the control of an unseen

force. There was nothing mechanical supporting me, yet my perceptions confirmed that I was there. A light source emanating
from somewhere overhead illuminated the trees. Its brightness lit
up the lush, green foliage beneath my drifting body and deepened
the depths of the spaces between the sweeping floor of leaves.

My original interpretation of that flying experience changed as
I became more familiar with alien abduction scenarios. What was
once remembered as a pleasant dream-flight, scheduled by the
unpredictable and imaginative workings of the dreaming mind,
eventually lost its label as "just a weird dream." It became part of
a thick, cognitive file filled with unexplained, but vividly remembered experiences that now carried the heading of "possible close
encounters."

Other odd dreams containing out-of-the-ordinary images were
added to that growing list as well. One time I saw a saucer-shaped
object hovering near the ground several yards away from some
railroad tracks. The setting was at night in an isolated area and
there was junk on the ground that looked like abandoned machinery or perhaps old railroad cars.

In another dream, I observed an alien creature whose body was
so unusual that I questioned how I was able to subconsciously
manufacture such a clever image. The alien form had features
that I had never comprehended before. Whatever covered its grayish body was rough and creased. Long, deep furrows ran up and
down the length of its torso, arms, and legs, giving the creature's
skin the appearance of wood bark. The peculiar figure was surprisingly thin. By human standards, it would have been described
as emaciated.

The area where I observed the curious creature was unfamiliar
to me, too. It was dark there, like night, a wooded, shadowy place.
Yet enough light found its way through the trees to illuminate the
odd figure.

The creature walked stooped over like a crippled old man,
straining against the weight of its own body, hesitating a moment

before attempting each step. The gaunt, gray form inched along a dirt path that gradually led upward and to the right, slowly lifting one bony leg in front of the other before cautiously setting it back down.

I was following the being's progress, watching it move away from me, when I suddenly became aware that the old and weary life form was dying. In that instant, a burst of emotion spread through me, filling my heart and my soul with a dense sadness. I wanted to run to the alien and comfort it, but the dream scene changed abruptly and I found myself standing in a different location.

The peculiar creature was now just a short distance in front of me. I gauged its height at about four feet. Between the gray being and the place where I stood was a two-foot high by three-foot wide circular nest containing several beige eggs. The top edge of the nest was neatly fashioned out of what appeared to be a layer of twigs, and the eggs were the size of ostrich eggs.

I continued to study the alien form as it labored to complete a couple more steps. Then it leaned over and climbed onto the nest. The creature spread its shriveled body over the eggs, carefully, gently, wrapping its skinny arms and legs underneath itself, assuming a posture that reminded me of a mother embracing a lifeless child. It remained there in that position, motionless, except for the slight heaving of its chest. I sensed that the alien creature was crying, though I saw no tears. It was waiting there to die and crying because it was leaving behind a part of itself it would never see.

My eyes remained fixed on that profound scene for several more seconds, the creature's sadness still clinging to me like a wet garment, weighing down what seemed like the very core of my life energy. Then the sad image faded away.

The day after I experienced that "dream," I walked around as if in a trance, and the heavy emotion I felt during the strange encounter remained inside my heart for a very long time. Whenever I thought about the creature, I felt sad. Tears would sometimes slip over the edges of my eyes, causing me to question how it was possible to feel such strong human emotion toward a form I did not even recognize. What was that thing, that bizarre creature? I would ask myself. Why did I feel so connected to it? It was foreign, alien, to me, I thought.

Still, its unusual features were similar to images of alien beings I had seen before, like the image that used to appear in my mind in the 1980s, long before I knew anything about alien abductions, but during the time when my broken sleep was often punctuated with the feeling that someone had entered my house. The image of that creature and the beings who showed up in my parents' bedroom were also covered in gray, or shades thereof, with bodies that were boxlike, rectangular, with long, skinny necks, arms, and legs attached. Their heads, if not covered with a queer hat, were bulbous, elongated and bald. What was especially unusual were the large, round eyes that stared straight ahead through solid blackness. The lack of any white space left you to wonder exactly where the eyes were directed, unless of course they were focused on you, and that could never be mistaken.

As for noses and ears, these were never prominent features and were not noticed as much as other, more obvious aspects, like the aliens' posture, for example. Their posture was definitely conspicuous. The alien beings I observed seemed to lean forward at a definite angle, giving them the carriage of little old men who might be suffering from osteoporosis.

Because of the many similarities between the alien figures seen as a child and later as an adult, it occurred to me that if I was manufacturing these strange creatures in my mind at least I was being consistent.

Another peculiar dream that I remembered from a time before I knew anything about the alien abduction phenomenon took place in a circular gray room. Like a sunken living room, it was terraced with four or five levels of steps that circled the center floor in a series of rings. These steps were about two feet wide and served as seating for the group of human strangers I observed while standing near the wall at the top of the terracing. Somehow I knew I was inside an alien spaceship, though that idea made little sense to me when I thought about the dream the next morning.

In addition to dreaming that I was inside an alien spacecraft, I could also remember seeing spaceships in the sky. Though I had never witnessed a confirmed UFO—not even an unconfirmed one, for that matter—many of my dreams displayed aerial devices that easily fit the popular descriptions of unidentified flying objects.

The spaceships I observed, however, varied in size, performance, and form. A few were shaped like a saucer, thicker in the middle than at the edges, while the majority appeared more triangular, with rounded edges like a sardine can cut diagonally in half. In the moments I observed them in daylight, I detected lines, tubular protrusions, and varying textures on the underbellies of the objects. Some were viewed at a distance, seen as a bright light moving around erratically like a firefly in the night sky. Others were not flying at all, but merely lingering in midair.

Whenever such craft were in sight, there typically was an unforgettable, almost transcendent quality to the overall experience, sort of a starry-eyed feeling that as a child compared to nothing in my realm of perception. That feeling made my spaceship dreams a complete mystery to me.

The mystery was further confounded by the fact that my childhood fantasies never centered on spaceships or aliens. Instead, my child-imagination seemed content with simple play, such as instigating a gallop-like hop while I ran around the farm, secretly pretending to be a horse. Even when I was older, my daydreams were typical of young girls: I wanted to look and sing like Leslie

Gore; I imagined meeting Paul McCartney. The fantasies I created in my imagination included people, places, and things found in reality—or perhaps seen on an album cover. They were not created out of what I believed then to be science fiction. I can't say that I never thought about UFOs or spaceships, only that the conceptual distance between the content of my childhood ruminations and the ideas bouncing around in my head during my alien dream encounters was extreme.

The most extraordinary example of this dichotomous mindset was an encounter that occurred when I was about ten years old. For me, that was still an age of simplicity and innocence, as farm life had a way of preserving those qualities.

The encounter took place while I was playing underneath the century-old maple tree that stood in the yard next to the farmhouse. During most of the year, the giant tree shaded the heavily used path that led from the house to the dairy barn. I frequently played in that space between the house and the barn, but one day I saw something through the maple tree's verdant branches that was both shocking and wondrously incredible. There in the sky, beyond the maple and over the cut hay fields that bordered the yard, sat a squadron of flat, triangular spaceships.

They seemed to appear out of nowhere, and like an animal that has discovered it's become something's prey, my body instinctively froze. At the same moment, my mind just went wild as it tried to comprehend what was there in the sky: at least fifteen spaceships, maybe more, mysterious, silent, and gray. They hung weightless in the air, watching, waiting for something to happen. Then a lightning-quick flash of fear swept through my body, engraving the unbelievable image into memory for all time.

I shifted my eyes from the sky toward the ground and gauged the distance between where I stood and the house. Could I make it if I ran? I wondered, while the comforting image of my mother took shape in my mind.

But as swiftly as fear overtook me, a wave of pure joy rushed in to take its place. It flooded the very center of my being in an instant, effecting a complete change of mind and a total reversal of emotion.

I turned and lifted my head to again view the ships, but by this time the fear had completely washed away. Instead of wanting to run toward the house and toward the protective arms of my mother, my mind was suddenly filled with knowledge about the people inside the spaceships. I knew who they were in that instant, and I was overcome with joy and excitement at the prospect of being with them again. I also knew why the ships were there in the sky.

As that awareness sprouted, other knowledge flowed into my mind, knowledge that contained concepts far beyond anything my ten-year-old mind had ever held before. Those concepts seemed to hold great significance and meaning for my life. But hours later, when I reflected on the experience, that magnificent knowledge— as if a gift, I recall—was no longer within my mental reach.

The only specific thoughts that remained in memory were formed around a curious question. As I stood under the maple tree in the yard, viewing the spaceships as they hovered over the farm fields, the following thought filled my mind: How will the world react? I was concerned about how the world would react to the arrival of alien aircraft. That issue gravely concerned me. I distinctly remember focusing on that one, single question as if it were critical to the future of the world. Within the time it took to complete a breath, my state of mind shifted from fear for my personal safety to a calm, philosophical debate as to whether or not the world was prepared to see what was there before me.

With my eyes still fixed on the gray, hovering shapes, I addressed the people I seemed to know in the ships, "No," I said, telepathically. "The world is *not* ready!"

The child that I was in the mid-1960s was content to define that bewildering experience as merely a fantastical dream. However, my memory of the strange aircraft and the peculiar transformation that came over me during the encounter was magnified by a factor of two when a year later I experienced a repeat encounter.

The second "dream" unfolded exactly as the first, only I was walking up the gravel road that runs past the yard in front of the house when I first spotted the silent spaceships. The same gray, flat, triangular objects appeared again out of nowhere, but this time they were positioned over a different section of fields. The ships hung at varying heights up ahead and to the right from where I stood on the road.

My initial reaction to the sight of the spaceships mirrored that of my previous encounter: sudden, paralyzing terror. The vast number of machines in the sky alone heightened their formidable presence. And once again my initial thought was to run, to sprint toward the house and to safety, though I was certain that such an attempt would be futile; the distance was too great.

But I never found out if it was too great. I never had the chance to escape. My emerging sense of helplessness never completely evolved, because in the blink of an eye I became someone else again, someone far different from the terrified eleven-year-old girl who was standing on the road.

Once again, my fear dissolved into pleasure as another reality burst full and bright into my awareness. Just as the encounter had played out the year before, I knew things in that moment that seemed to explain it all: why the ships were there in the sky, their purpose, as well as my purpose. That overwhelming, wonderful knowledge brought me joy and contentment. The feeling was absolute bliss. It felt like a homecoming, a celebration of minds connecting after a long time apart.

As a young girl, I probably replayed those two baffling experiences over in my mind a hundred times, searching for their meaning, longing to remember some small bit of information from within the vast store of knowledge that returned to me while the gray ships stood watch overhead. It seemed as if I had remembered something vitally important, something that was fundamental to my existence. Whatever it was, the spark of it filled me with recognition, elation, and hope. While looking upward toward the spaceships, the recognition was certain and the elation was intense. And during the years that followed, the feeling of hope always drew me back to reflect on the experience.

Those two mysterious sightings had a profound effect on me, especially as a child, and the enduring feelings associated with the experience would sometimes bring tears to my eyes, even to my adult eyes. The tears came in response to the haunting emptiness that remained with me through the years. I felt empty because I could never recall the knowledge that had filled me with such joy and peace while I stood in the presence of the alien ships.

Still, I never forgot that once as a young girl I knew something that seemed almost magical, and when exploring the alien abduction phenomenon and reading the bizarre accounts of alien contact, a hint of that magic returned. But it never stayed with me for more than an instant. Disbelief and fear always chased it away.

As a child, I readily accepted what I couldn't understand, but as I grew older, I started to build walls of resistance against the unknown. By the time I was an adult, a fortress separated me from anything magical or out of the ordinary, even if I suspected it was real.

CHAPTER 4

Anxious Days and Sleepless Nights

As you continue to breathe into the body, you continue to go deeper and deeper," I heard Gary Dallek say, "and as you go deeper, all feelings, thoughts, and sensations continue to move you deeper."

The reins controlling my consciousness were beginning to slip out of reach, and my mind, which had been speeding away from the present, was now galloping off in an unknown direction. I knew I was still sitting in the leather recliner, and I knew Mr. Dallek was still seated at my side, yet my awareness was separating from the physical realm around me, racing off toward points unknown within the regions of mental space.

"As you go deeper, there's a certain feeling growing stronger and stronger, more and more powerful, a feeling growing stronger, a thought growing stronger, a sensation growing stronger and stronger, more and more powerful, as you move deeper, going deeper now."

When Mr. Dallek spoke of feelings, of thoughts, of sensations, his words suddenly seized the reins, and my awareness was pulled back for a moment to recall a part of reality that I would have preferred to leave behind. Looming in that conscious dimension were feelings of fear, sensations of anxiety, and the expectancy that aliens or other strange beings would suddenly appear during the night—the fallout from a lifetime of frightening encounters, with my unexpressed emotions still attached. That was the place where I hid my silent screams.

Nearly a year had passed since I'd peered into that realm, and the last time I went looking for old memories, a door was slammed in my face. I was resting on my bed, meditating, taking a mental journey back in time. I had gone back to rural Wisconsin, back twenty years, to review what happened on the night I heard someone walking across the Pritchards' kitchen, the night I saw the gray, alien face.

With my eyes softly closed and the lights in my bedroom turned down low, I searched my mind for that old memory. I could still hear the sound of the dog barking. I could still see the sweep of unexplained lights streaming through the curtains covering the window in the living room. I could still remember walking down to the side entrance to unlock the doors, then back up to the living room to look out the window again. The night view across the field and toward the main road was still there in my memory, too. Another trip to lock the side doors for the second time, and then I was back on the couch.

At that point in my memory, I drew a deep breath because I knew what was coming up next: the awful sound of bodies shuffling around in the entryway, followed by the pad of mysterious footsteps across the kitchen floor. But at the height of horror, when I saw myself standing in the middle of the living room, wrapped in dread, waiting for something to happen, I suddenly screamed, "S-t-o-p!"

I sprang up into a sitting position, covering my face with my hands. My heart was racing, my head was spinning, and my stomach had turned upside down. I felt like every cell in my body was about to erupt. I was having a panic attack, and it caught me completely off-guard.

Only a moment before, I was lying on my bed feeling calm and relaxed, simply exploring the past in my mind's eye. I had no idea that I was peering inside a Pandora's box, or that its contents could have such power over my emotional and physical well-being.

Nevertheless, I found what I had gone looking for. The alien face was still there in my mind, where it had been for so many years. But there was something else, too, something I remembered but didn't want to see. In the flash of revisiting the alien's timeless image, and at the moment I screamed "Stop!" I had seen the ashen, unearthly creature step out from behind the wall and come toward me.

Something else *had* taken place in the Pritchards' living room many, many years before. I was sure of it, but my unconscious mind was apparently not ready to give up the entire secret, at least not yet. It would only let me see the strange gray face and permit a fleeting glimpse of the alien as it came into full view. Still, I knew something very real, something very frightening had found its way into the Pritchards' house, and I couldn't help but wonder if it had come looking for me.

My horror at seeing the alien actually step out from around the corner brought back to mind my strange reaction to the alien I remembered from one particular scene in the movie *Communion*. I compared both scenes in my mind. There was something unforgettable about the way the alien in the movie and my alien visitor had leaned out into view. It was the combination of silent, sinister, and cautious.

Curiosity prompted a search through the pages of Whitley Strieber's *Communion* for his actual description of the alien being who peered out at him. When I located that scene in the book, I was surprised to discover that there was a similarity between Strieber's unannounced visitor and my surprise guest that I failed to note during my initial reading of the book:

I could see perhaps a third of the figure, the part that was bending around the door so that it could see me. It had a smooth, rounded hat on, with an odd, sharp rim that jutted out easily four inches on the side I could see.[13] [Emphasis mine.]

One of the most enduring features to remain of the alien image I still held in memory was the peculiar hat the alien form was wearing. When the gray creature leaned out from around the corner, the hat's "sharp rim" partially covered the dark eyes that stared across the room into mine.

Remembering that hat, after concluding it had been a hallucination, made that conclusion even more unbelievable. If I had hallucinated the image, I questioned, why would I put an obtuse-looking hat on a fabrication? And, since I dream in color, why didn't my mind picture the illusion with human skin tones and produce a varying color for the hat? The entire image I perceived was a flat gray.

Experiencing a panic attack in the midst of reliving a twenty-year-old memory convinced me that the gray image I once perceived was no hallucination. Seeing the image again in my mind forced me to stare into the alien's face and recall the subtle look of surprise that the creature's eyes communicated to me. What I was looking at was certainly not human, but what I saw in the creature's eyes told me it was definitely a sentient being.

The skinny, gray creature had not only looked at me, it had stepped out from around the corner and moved toward me. The being seemed to come rushing at me. My memory of that moment was patchy, yet enough of it was there to assure me that I wasn't making it up, and the memory was inseparable from my emotion. The full image of the creature had produced a painful reaction, plus an involuntary scream that felt like a desperate plea: *Stop! Stop! Stop!*

I wondered if I had screamed at the alien as it advanced into the room, or maybe the word, along with the disbelief and terror, had been frozen into silence by the power of an alien mind. It had been suggested, both by researchers and abductees, that aliens did have the ability to cause amnesia. If true, it would explain why the alien, now seen coming around the corner, was seen twenty years ago vanishing into thin air. Of course, there was also the possibility that I had simply repressed a traumatic experience into my unconscious, a feat easily accomplished by the protective human mind.

The alien abduction phenomenon provided an explanation for many of my peculiar life events. Yet, I stood for a long time at the edge of objective reality, wondering how such a bizarre phenomenon could actually be real, even with my own alien-related experiences in plain sight. I no longer questioned the credibility of close encounter stories; I no longer doubted the probability that aliens were the strange creatures in my baffling "dreams." Still, I couldn't step completely into the region of belief.

Rationalizing that I was personally involved with aliens, and internalizing that reality as a belief were two completely different psychological processes. Rationalization required only logic, whereas adopting a new belief was a much more emotional event, especially when it required merging a mind-bending reality into a person's traditional belief system. It was like trying to force a square peg into a round hole while knowing that as long as both the peg and the hole remained in their original form nothing would ever fit. Something would have to change, or something would have to give way, and it was too late to go back to believing that aliens didn't exist.

Merging the reality of aliens and alien abductions into my belief system required a great deal of time. It also caused a tremendous amount of turmoil. My psyche writhed and strained as it struggled against the implications of that disturbing reality. At the same time, it searched for answers to a dozen new enigmas: Who are "the grays"? Where do they come from? Why have they targeted me? When will they come back?

I could not assume that my involvement with aliens had ended. My history with the creatures had covered thirty years. I knew it was only a matter of time before they would come looking for me again in the night.

Accepting that reality—that I would see the gray beings again— was the hardest part of all. The mere thought of experiencing another encounter sent me directly into denial, and I would say to myself: This can't really be happening to me; I can't be involved in something this strange, this bizarre; maybe there's another explanation for alien abductions. But then the image of the alien's face, slipping out from around the corner, would come back into view, violently shaking the foundation of my denial and forcing me to look once again into the alien's dark, mysterious eyes.

In the beginning, there was always conflict, conflict between what was emerging as a reality and what I struggled to believe. I knew I had experienced alien encounters long before I had any knowledge about gray aliens. I knew I was fully awake, standing on my feet, when one of those encounters occurred. And I knew I had looked straight into the eyes of a nonhuman being, a sentient being. Whenever any doubt or denial would return to cloud those facts, the alien eyes were always there insisting that I remember, challenging me to believe, and forcing me to accept as true that which seemed impossible.

Eventually, the square peg did fit into the round hole, but only after the hole—my world, my old reality—broke open and everything around it fell apart. Paradigms tumbled. Belief structures cracked and crumbled. I had to admit that even the laws and principles defining my physical world no longer applied, as aliens lived by different rules. These beings could appear without warning. They could walk through doors, through solid objects. Aliens could make you forget actual experiences, or disguise them as strange dreams so you would naturally assume they were created by your mind.

Embracing the reality that aliens truly existed suddenly turned the world into an unpredictable place. To believe in aliens and to believe that I was involved in the alien abduction phenomenon required that I accept my vulnerability to the aliens' schemes— whatever they were—and along with that, to never know when they might return. It took months, and finally years, to learn to live with that uncertainty.

Some days I would long to return to my former view of reality, to the simplicity of ignorance and to the security afforded by doubt. I thought that if I went back to believing that aliens were only dream figures and the spaceships in my dreams were merely reflections of a subconscious mirage, then I could go back to living in a safe and predictable reality. That reality had served me well for over thirty years, and a part of me did not want to give it up. I wasn't ready to leave my old views behind and start playing a different life game, especially one with such unfamiliar boundaries and odd, eccentric rules. I wasn't prepared to play alien hide-and-seek, knowing that I could never really hide and that aliens seemed to play by their own rules, where anything goes. As a result, I continued to vacillate back and forth between accepting my involvement in the alien abduction phenomenon and denying any association with it.

Acceptance; denial. Denial; acceptance. I straddled those two mindsets for many months, keeping one foot solidly planted in my old world while the other gingerly tested the footing just beyond my normal realm. That realm bordered on the fringes of reality, and except for ufologists and abduction researchers, few people were even exploring that uncharted region. The scientific community, as a whole, denounced the view that alien beings existed, always supporting their position with the question, "Where's the proof?" When the subject of aliens and abductions surfaced in the media, it was usually pulled down by a wave of controversy, and the froth left in the wake of UFO and alien debunkers made it extremely difficult for anyone to admit to having experienced alien contact or abduction without feeling like a freak.

Knowing how the alien abduction phenomenon was viewed by the scientific community and treated by the media only added to the burden of my changing beliefs. Clearly, it was easier to stand on the side of denial, and as I moved closer to acceptance, I realized it was safer to keep my new and evolving perspectives to myself.

There was stress, layers of stress, during the months I silently struggled with my conflicting mindsets, and there was always the desire to push the subject of aliens and abductions into a mental box and simply close the lid. But whenever I did, the gray, alien face would eventually pop up like a jack-in-a-box, forcing its way back into my thoughts, and with those dark, seeking eyes, the bobbing alien head would say, "So what are you going to do about it?"

What were my choices? I had already tried to dismiss my experiences as unexplainable unknowns. I had even given credence to the possibility that they were mentally induced apparitions, hallucinations. I had tried turning away from the entire matter, choosing to look the other way, ignoring the plaguing questions. Those solutions no longer worked. The only remaining option was to embrace the truth: I had been in the presence of aliens and the strange incidents that had bewildered and challenged my common sense for more than thirty years had arisen out of a realm beyond conventional norms. Intelligent, nonhuman life forms did exist, and they periodically interacted with me whether I wanted them to or not. What I had to do now was learn to cope with the uncertainty of alien encounters as well as the internal and external pressures associated with my changing beliefs.

During most of 1991, my approach to coping with the alien abduction phenomenon was to physically and mentally keep moving. By consciously filling my life, my days, my thoughts with my old reality—work, friends, romance, sports—I was able to stay within my familiar comfort zone. I felt safe there. I thought that as long as I stayed on the treadmill of normal life, running with the joys, demands, and stresses of day-to-day living, I could deal with a periodic glance into the aliens' unknown realm.

But in spite of maintaining a full and active social life and devoting large chunks of time to my business responsibilities, something peculiar found a way into my awareness and into my house. Though I lived alone, I started to feel and act as if I had an unseen visitor. I would be walking down the hallway, for instance, thinking about work or mundane things, when suddenly I would sense someone standing behind me. Instinctively, I would glance over my shoulder to see who was there, but always found an empty space. There were times though when I would stare into that space and sense that someone was still there, looking straight at me, just beyond my sight.

Whenever that eerie sensation occurred late at night, I would nearly go crazy. I started turning on the hallway, kitchen and living room lights during the evenings when my work continued into the early morning hours. I started to leave a light on in my bedroom at night before crawling under the blankets. I started to close my bedroom door before going to sleep, and on some nights, I would feel so uneasy that I actually locked my bedroom door, a precaution I'd never taken before. Even though I tried to convince myself that my behavior was baseless and that there was no need to feel insecure, I could not stop the anxiety from creeping up along my spine whenever I would sense that some unseen person was with me in the house.

And so began another nightly ritual that continued for about three months, dropping off in frequency thereafter, but resurfacing from time to time whenever that overriding sense of someone's presence invaded my house. Unlike previous rituals, however, this one did not involve looking under the bed, checking the closets, or surveying hidden spaces. I knew who was lurking in the shadows, and whether real or imagined, this type of entity would not be found hiding under the bed. Aliens didn't need to hide. If they could walk through solid objects, they could probably make themselves invisible, too.

Admittedly, I thought and worried too much about aliens, but there were periods when aliens were the last thing on my mind. Days and weeks could go by and my thoughts would be focused on work, deadlines, a new project, an old boyfriend, shopping, decorating, or taking time off to play. But I came to realize over time that when my conscious mind was absorbed in day-to-day activities, my subconscious was ever the dutiful sentinel, keeping watch in the night, and prompting me still to occasionally look over my shoulder.

That guardedness materialized unexpectedly one night in August of 1991. I had gone on vacation with Dick, a friend of mine whose family was gathering at a cabin near Lake Sakakawea in North Dakota. Dick, his brother Don, and I stayed at a small motel in a nearby village. During the week, we traveled back and forth over the few miles between the cabin and the motel.

One evening, well after midnight, and on a return trip to our motel, the three of us noticed that the sky was ablaze with pulsating color. Beaming up from the horizon and over the North Dakota plains was the aurora borealis. I had seen this phenomenon before, but never as brilliant or with shades of purple and green mixed into the lights that ebbed and flowed across the sky.

"Stop the car," Dick commanded, obviously excited at seeing such a spectacular sight. "Let's get out for a better look." The brothers quickly exited out the front doors of the vehicle. My door, however, remained closed.

"Come out here, Janet," one of the guys said, but I didn't want to, not after realizing where we had stopped. The car sat on a dark country road with nothing but farm fields on either side. Immediately, I felt anxious, afraid. Even the huge expanse of sky, in all of its brilliance, communicated a threat to me. The three of us were now sitting ducks on an open field, totally vulnerable to the night, to the unexpected appearance of aliens.

"No," I said as calmly as I could. "I can see fine from here. Really." But I wanted to say, "Please get back into the car. Let's go. Let's get out of here. At least close your damn car doors." I thought about lunging over the front seat and pulling the open doors shut, but that would have required a bit of explaining.

Dick and Don continued to view the aurora borealis while standing in the cool country air. As for me, my eyes searched out across the open fields, scrutinizing every silhouette, every shadow, then across the sky to scan for moving lights. My mind was inflating with fear, and the fear swelled until it infected my body. The muscles in my arms and legs tightened and tightened until the men finally climbed back into the car and we pulled away. Only then was I able to quiet myself, taking slow, deep breaths, while we traveled the remaining miles to the motel.

It was amazing how quickly my mind could slide into a pool of fear, even with little or no provocation. The fear would be instant. It felt organic, as if it had a life all its own. I couldn't control it. The fear would just happen, and though I wasn't counting the times, I knew it was happening more and more frequently. Even trips back to the family farm in Wisconsin were triggering panic attacks.

I seldom had any trouble navigating my emotions through the daylight hours while at the farm, but once the sun set below the horizon, shrouding the woods, the fields, the farm buildings, and the house in thick shadows of night, my senses switched over to an internal, unconscious radar. During the night, any unusual sound in the house broke my sleep. The slightest outdoor disturbance—a cow bellowing, a dog barking, a pig squealing, a cat hissing—would bring me around to consciousness. But it was waking into absolute silence that frightened me the most. Like the calm before the storm, such perfect stillness was abnormal, it threatened of an impending fate—small bodies appearing, physical paralysis, the rising fear, then blackout. My psyche reacted to the dead quiet of night as if it were a preternatural state, cautioning me to be on guard, to be watchful.

Turning my mind back toward sleep under such conditions was usually a waste of time. I would lie awake for hours, vigilantly monitoring the night sounds, the shadows around the bed, and the place in my mind that signaled when something strange was about to happen. I had learned to know that place, that awareness, as a small child and while in the same room where I slept when visiting the farm as an adult. That bedroom was also where I had slept during the years of my recurring childhood nightmare and the mysterious trips I took into the woods.

Regardless of where I spent my nights though, — whether in new places, old familiar haunts, or even in my own home in the city — I never knew when the anxiety and panic would strike again. It seemed that the disposition of my fears was extremely unpredictable and, like a schoolyard bully, hard to avoid or bring down. Still, there were days when I believed that I had brushed all fear aside or at least buried my fears under reason and common sense. I would be in control of my emotions again, and think that it was safe to go on with life and stop worrying about placing myself in vulnerable positions.

Days and weeks might go by, then from around a corner the fear would jump out and ruthlessly punch me in the stomach, letting me know that my apprehension about being abducted and seeing small, gray creatures again had only been lying in wait. By the time I discovered that my fears had stepped into the ring for another round of boxing, it was too late to throw in the towel. I would already be buckled over, writhing in terror, with no place to hide and no allies in sight. My panic attacks quickly bled out as despair, because I knew there was no escape and no protective cover when aliens were promoting the fight.

A trip I took with my cousin Sheila Castleberg in October 1991 was a perfect example of my psyche's fragility during a time when I felt emotionally strong and secure. What was meant to be a relaxing vacation turned out to be an endurance test for anxiety.

Sheila and I headed off toward Door County, one of Wisconsin's attractions to tourists, artists, and nature lovers, to spend a week in Ellison Bay. Sheila was going to paint, as she had registered for a watercolor class at The Clearing, a learning center designed to enable adults to "clear" their minds. My plan was to spend the week hiking and biking near the cabin I had rented and sit in front of a cozy fire at night reading books.

The hours of driving time flew by as my cousin and I talked our way across the state of Wisconsin, filling each other in on the details surrounding our families, our work, our pastimes, and our personal lives. It was late in the afternoon by the time we completed the last leg of our journey, traveling northward up the state's peninsula to our final destination at its tip. We were both excited to be off on another adventure together and looking forward to a change of pace, hopefully slower that the ones we left behind.

After taking Sheila's luggage to her room at The Clearing, we navigated the country roads, lined with fruit orchards and the vestiges of a simple way of life, until we found the cabin I had rented. It was rustic, but perfect. The woodbox next to the fireplace was filled with logs, the country kitchen was fully equipped, and the two bedrooms were spacious and warmly decorated. The cabin sat among birch, pine and oak, actually an entire forest of growing things that shielded it from the likes of civilization. During daylight, that setting was a city dweller's paradise, but during the night, it became an alien abductee's hell.

Hours later, after Sheila was back at The Clearing, I marked my place in the book I'd been reading and looked around me. The logs in the free-standing fireplace had burned down to a few glowing embers. Before I had realized it, darkness had moved in.

I sat for a while, just thinking about where I was, and then the reality of my location suddenly sank in. I was sitting on the edge of the world, from a terrestrial perspective, at least. I was on the tip of a peninsula, with nothing but water surrounding me—Lake Michigan—and only one road leading out. I looked around the darkening cabin, conscious that I was alone and about to go to sleep in a cabin, in the woods, in the middle of an enormous lake, and it was pitch dark outside. But after years of experience, I knew exactly what to do.

I set about to secure the hatches—locking doors, fastening windows, pulling down the shades, drawing the curtains. I dragged the weighty woodbox that sat in the entryway, filled with life jackets and other boating gear, across the back door. Once in my bedroom, just before turning off the lights, I set up another line of defense. I dragged the chair that was sitting in the corner over to the door to serve as a barricade. I was taking no chances.

By the time I crawled into the double bed, my fear had already risen to heart level. I remember lying under the blankets thinking about how much I resented the feeling that had suddenly consumed my sense of adventure and the fun in being someplace new. It had even devoured the reassurance I felt in knowing that the owners of the cabin and a few other residents were easily within walking distance. "God, how I *hate* feeling like this!" I exclaimed in the middle of the night, wishing that I could just fall asleep.

But sleep never came. The stillness of the night, the darkness around me, and the isolation of the cabin overwhelmed the nocturnal rhythms of my brain. I tried to find something soothing to think about, but I kept returning to the thought that I was alone and that aliens somehow seemed to know that about the people that chose to abduct.

I watched the hands of the electric clock slowly circle toward morning, and all the while my anxiety level kept building and building until my nervous system nearly burned itself out. With the physiology of my body stuck in high gear, I knew it was hopeless to try to sleep. Instead, I turned on the lamp that sat on the mirrored dresser and spent the rest of the night guarding myself, armed only with my open eyes.

By five o'clock, the morning sun had delivered a weak ray of light, but it was a ray of relief to my weary mind and body. It assured me that it was now safe to sleep, and I drifted off into unconsciousness for several hours. Sleep was mine at last.

When I saw Sheila later in the afternoon, I begged her to spend the rest of her nights at the cabin with me. She readily obliged, and during the week, she commuted to her painting class.

The double bed in the cabin was never slept in again. I chose instead to sleep in the same room as my cousin, in the twin next to her twin bed. I felt more at ease there, less frantic about my safety, with Sheila resting only four feet away and well within sight.

If aliens ever found me while I was tucked away in the woods, they made it their secret. No encounters took place—none that I could remember, anyway. Yet something did happen on the third night at the cabin that was peculiar and remained unexplained.

I woke up around 2:00 a.m. and saw a strange form slowly spinning in front of my eyes. It looked like a layer of mist between me and the solid objects I could see beyond my bed. The shadowy form was twirling in a counterclockwise direction, and after a few seconds, it shifted and started to circle in a clockwise direction. I was able to study the curious phenomenon for several seconds before it gradually faded from view.

I passed off the experience as "just another strange occurrence," only to be reminded of it later during the day when I opened the curtain over the window that was next to my bed. The interior window was closed and locked, but the inner glass plate that covered the exterior screen was more than halfway open.

I stared at the window, wondering how that could be, since I had made a serious inspection of all the windows just days before, closing and locking every layer of glass. The owners had not been inside the cabin, and Sheila confirmed that she had not opened any windows either. The open window remained a mystery, and it bothered me that the source of that mystery was located only two feet from my bed.

As lovely as Wisconsin's peninsula turned out to be, and as much as I enjoyed Ellison Bay and the rustic and comfortable cabin, I returned to Minneapolis from my vacation seriously in need of some sleep.

In retrospect, I should have sought professional help in understanding my alien-related experiences at the first sign of anxiety. Instead, I chose to deal with them on my own, keeping my conclusions about the past to myself, allowing the alien abduction phenomenon to become a secret part of my world. It wasn't until the anxiety had matured into debilitating forms (i.e., sleep disturbances, phobic behaviors, panic attacks) that I decided it was time to take action.

Not knowing exactly where to turn for help, I went to talk with a friend of mine who was also a practicing psychiatrist. I knew David would offer some form of advice, even if he didn't believe me.

"What's going on with you?" David asked, as we settled into places on his living room couch. He was obviously curious about my desire to get together and talk. I had been reluctant to give him an explanation when we spoke on the phone, stating only that I needed his advice on a personal matter.

I cautiously opened a discussion around the alien abduction phenomenon, pointing out along the way how I was involved and the emotional and physical impact it was having on me.

"I'm waking up usually between one-thirty and two in the morning," I explained to David. "It's now happening almost every night. When I wake up, my heart is pounding. I'm sometimes in a sweat. I feel terrified. It's not a gradual experience. I wake up like that, my entire body out of control. I'm completely wrapped in fear."

"How long has this been going on?" David inquired.

"On and off for several months, but lately it's happening more often, and because of that, I'm often exhausted. I can't get back to sleep after I wake up. I'm too anxious, too nervous. It's messing up my life. I'm having to take naps to get through the day. I feel like the night has turned into my enemy."

David searched through my situation, posing a variety of questions, including if I had suffered from sexual abuse or physical trauma at any point in my life.

"I've already explored that possibility in my mind," I said, continuing to address the abuse issue. "I don't think physical or sexual abuse has anything to do with this. One of my friends even suggested that I might be overreacting to all of the posters in my neighborhood alerting the public to be wary of a serial rapist who has attacked several women in the uptown area. That's not what's behind my fears, either. Actually, I'd be glad if that was the cause for my anxiety; at least I could deal with that. There would be measures I could take to protect myself to avoid possible threat."

"So how would you describe your fears?" David asked.

"What I'm afraid of is not a human being. It's something that comes through a locked door. It stands over me while I'm lying in my bed. I'm afraid because...I know this sounds bizarre...because these encounters really do happen, and I can't prevent them. They're totally unpredictable. The beings, the aliens, have never caused me any real harm. The truth is, when they're near me I'm usually not even afraid. The fear begins afterwards, when I remember that they were in my room in spite of a locked door, in spite of a locked window."

David listened intently, as an experienced psychiatrist would, allowing me to say what I needed to say. When I finished talking, he shared his position on the subject of alien abduction. He pointed out that although the psychiatric community had not formally embraced the phenomenon, he personally stood somewhere in the middle of the road.

"But whether alien beings are real or not doesn't matter at this point," David said. "What's important is that we get you back to sleep. You can't cope with your anxiety if you aren't getting any rest. You need to reestablish a normal sleeping pattern."

As an initial therapy, David recommended a week's supply of Xanax, a mild tranquilizer used to treat anxiety. He explained that the drug, if taken a few minutes before going to bed, would help me to relax and fall asleep.

"Our goal here is to break the pattern that is robbing you of a good night's sleep." David emphasized. "Once that's been done, we can explore this thing further, when you're feeling better, rested."

David also stressed the importance of not relying on drugs to induce sleep, and I assured him that I was not a "pill popper." But I was struggling with a condition unlike anything I had experienced before, so David's recommendation to take tranquilizers over a period of a few nights was worth a try. Actually, I would have been willing to try just about anything at that point to return to the nights when I would drift off to sleep within fifteen minutes of hitting the pillow, the nights when I didn't see the morning until it was time to get out of bed.

The tranquilizers did help me return to a sleeping routine that was far better than the one invented by my anxiety, even though I still woke up on and off during the night. If that happened while I was under the influence of the tranquilizer, I would look around my bedroom out of habit, and with a spunky, intoxicated attitude, I would address the aliens, saying, "Oh, so what! Come and get me." Within a few minutes, I would gently slip back into sleep. But if the drug's calming effects had worn off, as experienced later in the morning, the familiar pangs of anxiety would return and prevent me from returning to sleep. I quickly learned to take the medication just before going to bed so it would remain in my system throughout most of the night.

The transitory nature of my problems with anxiety, both before taking the tranquilizers and after, allowed me to think that I could manage and eventually overcome this annoying, though fleeting, psychological challenge. Days and sometimes even weeks would pass without any emotional uprisings during the night. These breaks would allow my sleep patterns to gradually return to normal, and the added rest would renew my energies and my ability to hold down my fears.

There were even occasions when I could actually examine the details of my alien encounters in my mind or read a book about the subject and still keep anxiety at bay. Then, without warning, it would strike again—the fear, the uncertainty, the feeling that I would never be safe. At times, that collection of angst would sneak up and grab me so suddenly that my reactions would not only surprise me, but also the people around me.

The first time that happened I was in the arms of a man.

Keith and I were introduced by our mutual friends, the Kleins, in 1986, shortly after I had moved to Phoenix, Arizona. Keith lived in Chicago, but had grown up near Phoenix, and he frequently returned to spend time with his family and friends. When I moved back to Minneapolis three years later, Keith and I maintained a casual friendship for several more years.

During the spring of 1992, it happened by chance that both Keith and I were back in Arizona. We met for dinner at the Kleins. Our hosts, however, were new parents, and shortly after dinner they put their new baby to bed and then turned in for the evening themselves, exhausted, as new parents often are. Keith and I, the vacationers, had to entertain ourselves.

We spent much of that evening soaking in the outdoor spa, watching the night produce a star-filled sky, while we updated each other on our lives and disparate careers: commodities trading versus corporate training. The bottle of wine we toasted the desert with was close to empty by the time our conversation shifted toward reminiscences of our shared past, and the past in general. Somehow, the subject of odd, unexplained events came up in the conversation, and that led me into telling Keith about my alien encounters.

Keith was keenly interested in what I had to say, and eventually I started to tell him about the night I heard footsteps in the Pritchards' house. I slowly mapped out the details that led up to my frightening encounter—the dog barking, the strange light, the locking and unlocking of doors, the footsteps, the disbelief. And emotionally I was fine up to that point; I hadn't felt even a twinge of anxiety. But as soon as I started to describe the alien's face, the fear returned and some repressed emotion unexpectedly gave way.

"I saw a face. It was gray. The face was gray," I told Keith. "Whatever was there in the kitchen, it leaned out from behind the wall. It looked at me. It just looked at me. I was standing there, but...but...oh, God, I can't move." At that moment, I stood once again in the Pritchards' house, pulled back through time to experience myself standing in the middle of the living room.

Tears suddenly spilled down over my checks, mixing with the water from the spa. I buried one side of my face into Keith's wet chest and wailed, "It's coming toward me, but I can't move. I c-a-n't m-o-v-e!"

Like a huge, unexpected wave, a wall of fear washed over me, and I felt as though I'd actually been knocked off my feet. Knowing it was useless to fight it, I allowed my mind to be buffeted by the power of my emotion until my psyche found its footing again.

I cried for awhile in Keith's arms, sobbing like a child, gasping every few seconds to fill my lungs with more air. I lingered there on purpose, emotionally out of control, taking comfort in the solid arms around me. Then, as the fear drained away, I slowly straightened my posture to let Keith know that I had regained my composure.

It was this flip-flopping back and forth between normal emotions and emotional extremes that gradually eroded my personal sense of well-being. Breaking down into tears was one thing, but completely crumbling in mind, body, and soul, if even for a few minutes, was not typical of my behavior. Something was changing me, and I didn't like the result.

As far back as I could remember, I had sustained a mostly calm, relaxed attitude about my life. There were, of course, periods of stress and times of uncertainty. My siblings still remind me that I was a moody adolescent, but at least the behavior fit the age. And after leaving the comfort and simplicity of my rural home, I sometimes found college, living in the city, and being on my own rather stressful. Then there were the years after college, filled with changing jobs, careers, relationships, and friends, years of trial and error. Still, during all that time the actual foundation of my being—my inner strength, my positive outlook, my belief in myself—never wavered for more than a few days or a week at a time, and I always returned to my center, to that inner core that defined "me."

But now I was struggling with something totally new, and it was wearing down my emotional stability, my confidence, even my physical health. Stress, anxiety, and fear were to blame. Under normal conditions, I could have coped with all three. But rooted as they were in events from the past, with some events half-hidden from view, they were not only unpredictable, but extremely powerful, too.

As more details of what actually took place in the Pritchards' living room surfaced, more of the unspent, pent-up terror attached to those details surfaced as well. It seemed as if my mind was slowly releasing images that it had locked away for safekeeping. Whatever I experienced that night while babysitting for the Pritchards must have been so terrifying that my psyche walled it off in the way that the human mind can. Or maybe the alien was responsible for my partial amnesia.

Regardless of how I forgot or why I was now remembering something that happened more than twenty years ago, a more important concern was my deteriorating sense of well-being. It was becoming apparent to me that I needed some support to help me through this difficult time.

I started to rehearse how I might approach the subject of aliens with Rita, one of my closest friends. She and I had been roommates during the mid-1980s, and our mutual backgrounds in education and our proclivity toward the outdoors, intrigue, and creative fun cemented our friendship for all time. Rita was one of my most open-minded friends, so I wasn't worried about her reaction to a discussion on aliens or how she would respond to my telling her that I was involved in the alien abduction phenomenon. The reason I had avoided sharing this aspect of my life with a woman who knew nearly everything else about me was knowing that it would change the future.

I knew that once I "came out of the closet" about my experiences, there would be no turning back. I could never occasionally lose myself in my old beliefs, or pretend that what I feared most wasn't real, because the people around me would know about my alien encounters, and they would want to talk about them. If I confessed my fears, my friends would worry about me. They'd either worry about my safety or worry that I'd lost my mind, depending on their beliefs about aliens.

When I finally spoke to Rita about my peculiar experiences, the conversation did not follow the script I had loosely rehearsed. I broke down in tears in the middle of it, and then words just gushed out. Rita and I were talking on the telephone when the subject of aliens came up. We talked for nearly two hours, and by the end our conversation I was sobbing, sobbing over the distress I felt because I sometimes couldn't sleep, sobbing because my fears were slowly taking control of my senses.

Rita neither judged me nor tried to convince me that my experiences were not what I believed them to be. She just let me unload the burdens of my secret life in the company of a compassionate friend. She mostly listened, but asked questions and consoled me, too. Then toward the end of our conversation, Rita emphasized two points that I needed to hear. Her words grounded my fears and her wit positioned my situation in a much more comfortable light. "The aliens have never caused you any permanent harm," Rita reminded me. "And remember, they always bring you back."

A short while later, I shared my history of alien encounters with another one of my close friends, Michelle. She, too, was open-minded and full of questions. Both Rita and Michelle suggested that I spend the night at one of their houses whenever I felt uncomfortable in my own home, and there were nights when I took them up on their offers. My anxious days and sleepless nights, though, were far from over.

But after more than a year of struggling to cope with the stress and anxiety that snaked in and out of my world, and after months of going to bed in fear of waking up during the night to find uninvited guests in my room, I decided that I wanted my simple, uncomplicated life back. I was tired of worrying. I was just tired of being tired, and stressed out all of the time. My fears were becoming old and trite, and I was weary of being victimized by them. Playing the victim had been a new role for me, and I didn't want to get good at it. Something in my life had to change, and I knew that the only way that was going to happen was if I took definite action to change it.

Determined to gain back my freedom from fear and anxiety, I developed a new and more aggressive strategy: I would declare war on aliens; I would chase them out of my life and my thoughts forever. Emotionally, I was ready to do battle with my nonhuman foes, but I needed an ally to effect my plan, someone skilled in dealing with the unknown.

I found that ally in Gary Dallek.

CHAPTER 5

Other Dimensions, Other Selves

ALL FEELINGS, THOUGHTS, AND SENSATIONS will continue to move you deeper here today. And as you go deeper, you breathe into the body, and there's a certain feeling growing stronger and stronger, more and more powerful."

The sound of Gary Dallek's voice continued to perform its magic, lulling me deeper into a smooth hypnotic trance, while his words directed my mind to perform a few effortless tasks. I was guided along a path of simple, unhurried discovery, and nothing I heard or saw during the next hour and a half seemed forced or falsely conceived. I was actually surprised at the ease in which complicated and colorful images appeared in my mind's eye. Even more surprising were the sounds and definable smells that sometimes accompanied the images.

I had no specific agenda while in this tranquil state, other than to end the painful pattern of fear and anxiety that had surfaced with my memories of aliens and spaceships and moments captured while staring into the eyes on a gray, alien face. I only wanted to end the fear that would sneak up on me in the middle of the night; I only wanted to feel in control of my emotions again.

Mr. Dallek, on the other hand, did have a plan. I was not entirely sure how he would accomplish this, but he told me before the hypnosis session that he would create a situation in which I could confront the aliens. "You mean I can talk to them?" I had asked, stunned by the notion. But apparently that was what I was going to do. I decided to put my trust into Mr. Dallek's expertise and just go with whatever happened. I had to admit that my problem was unusual, so maybe it required an equally unusual approach. Still, for reassurance, I held on to something Mr. Dallek had said earlier about hypnosis: "The energy of hypnosis is not to validate a person's experience in trance. The purpose is to assist you to move to your own inner understanding as you perceive it. Your perceptions are your reality."

Mr. Dallek's approach to my problem was not to spend any time exploring my alien-related memories, which I thought he might do. Instead, he took me on an exploratory journey into my mind. My mind, however, delivered me into another dimension of reality where I found people—more specifically, other consciousnesses, other entities—waiting to speak with me. I quickly realized during this journey that my mind was prepared to lead the way, sometimes in a direction chosen on its own accord without any assistance from Mr. Dallek, and sometimes in direct opposition to his guidance.

"As you rest comfortably in your special place, knowing your body is perfectly supported in every way, I'd like you to imagine the outline of your physical body above you. Imagine that you are looking up into a mirror and the outline you see is the outline of your energy body. As you look up at the outline of your energy body, I'd like you to move from the top of your head down through your body and become aware of any area that is not perfectly clear, for everything within the outline of your body should be perfectly clear, except the things we need to look at here today." (Mr. Dallek was applying a mirror technique to prompt my subconscious mind to present information to me and to identify areas in the body that might hold clues to subconscious issues.)

As I listened to his directions, a part of my consciousness—the part of "me" still sitting in the leather recliner—was thinking that this process was rather peculiar. Yet another part of "me," the part of my awareness that had first drifted, then sped off into the unknown reaches of my inner mind, was standing in a dimly lit room, perceiving an odor that I recognized as incense. In front of me were thick walls of stone, with markings similar to the simple lines and figures of hieroglyphics either etched or painted on the walls.

The scene before my eyes reeked of a tomb, and it seemed as though I was there because Mr. Dallek had said only minutes before that we were going to a room of healing and knowledge. Apparently, I had traveled to such a place, as if my psyche knew exactly where to go. But when Mr. Dallek told me to lie down on a comfortable place, I suddenly felt confused. What I could see before me was not what I had expected. It was hardly a place where I would go to relax.

A short distance ahead was a stone slab, a huge rectangular piece of smooth rock, at least four feet by six feet. It was positioned in the center of the room, rising a foot and a half off the floor, and a young woman was already lying on the stone slab.

Assuming that the person was me, I walked over to the woman and my mind moved effortlessly down into her body, as if that were the natural thing to do. The rock surface was cold and damp, yet I was quite comfortable and relaxed while lying on the stone slab. From that position, I observed the outline of my physical body above me.

"As you go deeper, you breathe into the body, and there's a certain feeling growing stronger and stronger, more and more powerful, your awareness of that feeling growing stronger and stronger, more and more powerful. And as you breathe into the area of the body that holds that feeling, that energy, your awareness grows stronger and stronger, more and more powerful. And whenever I touch your chin like this (he tapped the tip of my chin), it's a signal to the subconscious mind to bring forth verbal material, to bring forth knowledge in verbal form. If there are energies in the body that need to communicate, they can do so. What area of the body holds the energy of the intent that needs attention? Voice can speak free and clear."

"Spleen," I said, though in a confused way. I blurted the word out before my mind even had a chance to consider Mr. Dallek's question. Its sudden slip between my lips caused me to wonder who had spoken it. It seemed as if someone else had usurped my cognitive authority and had answered without asking for my approval.

"Breathe into the spleen. Take a deep, deep breath, and as you breathe into this area of the body, go deeper, breathing deeper. As you breathe into the spleen, your awareness grows stronger and stronger, and as you breathe into this area of the body, become aware of the color of the energy there. What color is the energy as you breathe into the spleen?"

I did not expect to find anything unusual when I scanned across the image of my body, but something was definitely there. A small section of pink was recognizable within the otherwise clear space. I reported to Mr. Dallek what I saw.

"Breathe into the pink," he said. "Energy of pink growing stronger and stronger in your awareness, more and more powerful, stronger and stronger, more and more powerful, stronger and stronger. And become aware of the first word, thought, or feeling that emerges out of the pink."

"Viva," I said. The response was immediate, and again it felt as though someone else was speaking for me.

My mind raced ahead to search for an explanation, but it stopped in mid-stride when I suddenly sensed another woman sitting confidently in the leather recliner, almost defiantly waiting for the next question. Her presence within me was somehow illuminating my mind, and it seemed as if I could access her thoughts, her awareness, her knowledge. From that source—wherever it came from—I knew that the presence, the consciousness that had joined me in the chair was also the woman on the stone slab, and her name was Viva.

"We're going to move back in time along the pathway of this energy called Viva to a few moments before it was ever a part of you. All time is open and available to you. As we move back along the path of this energy, it will continue to grow stronger and more powerful as you move back through time. Please allow that. As I count from ten down to one, moving back, flowing back, moving back. Nine. Moving back, flowing back. Eight. Moving back through time. Seven. Six. Moving back, flowing back. Five. Four. The energy growing stronger and stronger. Three. Two. On the count of one, be there in your mind. One. Be there now. Is it daytime or nighttime?"

"Nighttime," I said.

"Indoors or outdoors?"

"Indoors."

"Now I want you to look down at your body and become aware of how it appears to you. Look down at your body and tell me what you see."

I explained to Mr. Dallek that the woman lying on the stone slab didn't look like me. She had long, black hair that fell down around her shoulders and under her back.

"...and her eyes are blue," I added.

"Thank you. Now look down," Mr. Dallek instructed, "and describe what's covering the body."

"She isn't wearing anything," I said, feeling slightly embarrassed by the truth. "She's naked."

The woman's skin was light brown, and her body was petite. Though there was something familiar about her, I didn't recognize her face. All I was sure about was that the woman was the one called Viva.

"Let's move forward in time," Mr. Dallek prompted, "to the last few minutes of life in that physical body. I'm going to count from one down to three. Move forward as I count from one. Moving down. Two. Moving down to three. Be there now in your mind. Look down. Indoors or outdoors?"

"I'm in the same place...that darkened room," I said, aware that I was still in the ancient tomb where the naked female body remained motionless on the stone bed.

Then Mr. Dallek asked, "Why are you there?"

"I'm not sure, but I know that the woman...that...that I'm close to death," I said. "There's little life left in the body."

As that awareness swelled into my consciousness, a procession of dark-skinned, black-haired men—they were short, so perhaps they were boys—entered the room through its only opening. Their arrival introduced an air of pageantry within an otherwise solemn scene, and the ornamented wood stretcher resting on the shoulders of the two rows of bare-chested men suggested their purpose: to transport Viva's body to another place.

The entire scene was definitely cast from some earlier time. Though my historical knowledge of ancient Egypt was restricted to what I had learned in history classes, museums, and from an exhibit or two, such a time and place was my only reference to explain the dark and damp setting that had emerged from my mind. I wasn't fabricating the visual images and happenings seen there, but while describing my perceptions to Mr. Dallek, I felt a twinge of self-consciousness at my own report. The Egyptian theme was almost cliché in association with past life regression, and I hoped Mr. Dallek didn't think I was making up a story. I was only describing what had appeared in my mind's eye after Mr. Dallek had suggested that I go to a place of healing and knowledge.

Mr. Dallek gave me another instruction. "Move forward in time to a few moments after the physical body has died and float above your body. Look down and become aware of what's taking place."

I did not float above the body. Instead, I found that I was standing several feet back from the stone slab, watching a wispy, twirling cloud-like representation of the young woman rise up out of what was now the female corpse. As I described this to Mr. Dallek, the white cloud slowly faded from view, and so did the entire scene where I had been for the past several minutes.

Blackness now filled the screen directly in front of my eyes, and I sat for a short time staring into nothingness, hardly aware of Mr. Dallek's instruction to travel to a place of my choice. "Float forward slowly in time to see what happens next," he said.

A natural deep, slow breath swelled into my lungs, reminding me of the physical form that now barely contained me. The distance between my mind and my body seemed to expand with each intake of air, and as Mr. Dallek continued to tap on my wrist, I left more and more of that body behind. Sailing effortlessly through eternal time, a spirit wind lowered my essence down into a little boy.

I was walking through an orchard, where perfect rows of fruit trees displayed leafy branches that hung low to the ground. Stepping out into the sunlight, I noticed a wrought-iron fence towering well beyond my reach. I felt shorter than normal, at least shorter than I perceived myself to be, and I explained all this to Mr. Dallek, telling him that this was definitely not my female body.

I was wearing wool trousers, knickers, that ended just below the knee. A short-brimmed cap sat on my little-boy head, and I felt like smiling in response to my mood, a mood that belonged to a six-year-old boy. I seemed to know that was my age, along with the fact that I had been transported into the late 1800s.

Through the blackened rods of the iron fence and beyond a short stretch of yard, I could see a massive brick house. I regarded that place as my home, and in the next instant I was standing inside its brick walls, scrutinizing the oddly familiar surroundings.

A pleasant-looking young woman, probably in her early thirties, was standing behind a long table. She was wearing a white, high-collared blouse and a brown skirt that draped to the floor. The woman never looked up at me, apparently absorbed in her task of folding linens. Still, I recognized this person as my mother, and a rush of sweet emotion moved through me.

Behind the woman was a row of long, narrow windows that covered the full length of one wall, and treating the large, leafy plants positioned in various locations throughout the room was the natural light streaming in from the outdoors. I noted that the space was beautifully furnished and richly decorated.

I continued to describe to Mr. Dallek all that I saw and felt. Then he suggested that I move forward in time. When I did, it was only a tiny leap.

The woman I knew as my mother was now tucking me into bed. It was apparent that a strong, emotional bond connected me to her. I felt the strength and purity of that bond as the woman hovered above me to pull the bed covers across my small frame. The last thing I remembered before darkness invaded the scene was nuzzling my head into a fluffy, white pillow and feeling its softness against my young cheek.

"Horses. I'm seeing horses," I reported to Mr. Dallek. "They're running on a track. I'm at a horse race." A dramatic shift in awareness left me feeling as if I had literally been dropped into another human body. It was a man's body, and the momentary juxtaposition of the little boy's thoughts next to those of an adult male was curiously confounding.

A crowd of cheering spectators filled my view, and the raucous noise level coming from the stands instantly pulled me into the action taking place around me. My perspective of this scene, however, kept switching. One moment I'd be watching the horses or the people around me as if seeing them through the man's eyes. Then my perspective would shift, and I'd be several feet in front of the man, looking back at him.

When observing the man from a distance, I could see that he was wearing a long wool coat that buttoned up the front, and a gray fedora sat on his head. The man's coat and the garments worn by the men and women around him seemed appropriate for the early 1930s. I wondered if this man was the adult version of the child I had previously seen in my mind.

"Now move yourself forward in time. Move to the end of that life," Mr. Dallek directed.

Just as I saw the horses round the bend toward the finish line, the deafening roar of the crowd faded away, and in its place I heard Mr. Dallek's voice issuing yet another command: "Look around you and describe your surroundings."

"I'm in a bed," I said. "I'm old, really old. I see an old man with white hair. I am an old man." My point of view was shifting again, creating two separate perspectives that would flash back and forth in my mind. "And there are people next to the bed."

The varying heights of my bedside companions gave me the impression that there might be some children in the room. Looking up at these people, I was aware that their hearts were filled with emotion—heavy, sad emotion—because someone was leaving. I knew that person was me, but I did not share the grief spread across the faces staring down at my lifeless, wrinkled frame.

"If it is important to address those who are with you, or perhaps you simply wish to communicate your thoughts or feelings before you leave this life, do so now," Mr. Dallek said.

I paused for a moment to search for the words that appropriately captured the old man's thoughts. "Goodbye, my loving family," I said, noticing how the words airily waltzed on my breath.

Those words were cradled in a blanket of warmth, generosity, and contentment. Far away, I heard what seemed like an echo of the old man's emotions set into words: This has been a fulfilling life.

My perspective switched again, and I was no longer lying down, but standing somewhere near the doorway into the room. As I stood there, observing my family huddled near the bed, I saw that a white haze was coming out of the old man. It formed a small cloud that moved gracefully toward his feet, then it shot sharply upward to where it disappeared into the ceiling.

After I reported that event to Mr. Dallek, he spoke to me in a soft, assured tone, directing me to once again move forward in time. But I was already there, and I gasped in fear when I realized what had appeared before my eyes. Within seconds, tears were spilling down my face.

"They're, they're here. They're all around me," I whimpered, my voice barely audible. I had to force the words out through the vise clenching my throat. Shockwaves were racing down my spine and pulsating out to my extremities. Every muscle in my body was suddenly taut and bearing down.

"Who's there with you?"

"The gray aliens," I said, anchoring myself in the comforting sound of Mr. Dallek's voice. "They're standing all around me, surrounding me."

A part of me remained seated in the recliner, but another part was definitely somewhere else. I was standing far out in space, surrounded by a circle of four-foot aliens, my body frozen by a form of fear I knew only too well. All I could do was stare down on the aliens' bulbous grayish-white heads.

The instantaneous appearance of the gray beings completely erased the relaxed mood I was enjoying just seconds before. My body was now pushed deep into the chair's cushioned back, forced there at the demand of my rigid arms.

A thick coat of anxiety was swiftly spreading over my thoughts. I felt as if my mind had been plucked from one dimension and flown into another, but I had crash-landed in enemy territory. Now I was trapped with a group of aliens with only Mr. Dallek to help me find a way out. But rising up underneath the dread was my own voice reminding me that I was sitting in Mr. Dallek's recliner to face my alien foes. Hadn't I declared war on these intruders?

Apparently, they had accepted my challenge. But I never imagined that they would step into the middle of my hypnosis session and try to take control. Yet this unusual display—appearing out of nowhere, as if they were waiting for me all along—fit their tactical history. There was nothing that prepared a human being for abduction, either.

Mr. Dallek handled the situation with finesse. He diplomatically addressed the "little ones," either through me or directly, depending on whatever form of communication applied.

"Ask the little ones, the ones there with you, who they are," I heard Mr. Dallek say.

Communicating with the aliens came easily to me, probably because we had touched minds before. To address the beings, all I had to do was form a conscious thought, and project that thought out into mental space. When I would hear a response in my mind, usually in the form of one or two short phrases, I would then translate those phrases into words for Mr. Dallek's benefit. Sometimes I would sense an attitude in the aliens' responses that produced distinct emotions in me as the aliens' thoughts filtered down through my consciousness.

"They don't want to tell you," I said, summarizing my short dialogue with the aliens. While reaching into the invisible waves of mental thought and projecting Mr. Dallek's question into that space, I embraced a collection of sensations that I perceived as belligerent complacency. It was easy to separate my thoughts from those belonging to the aliens because they projected thoughts that produced feelings in me that were harsh and foreign.

"Where are you?" Mr. Dallek asked. "Look around and describe your surroundings."

"I feel like I'm just standing in space with these creatures all around me. I can't see anything beyond them. I'm just there. That's all." It appeared as if the aliens and I were standing in a fog, or a cloud, where the visibility extended no more than three or four feet.

Mr. Dallek gave me another instruction. "Ask the beings what their business is with you."

As I searched for a response, straining the aliens' mental projections through my mind, an overwhelming sense of arrogance and superiority surged through me. I felt like I was dealing with a group of insolent rebels, and it caused me to wonder if the aliens would ever cooperate with Mr. Dallek or with me.

"They're not telling me," I said, giving up hope of drawing out an answer. "It seems that they're preventing me from understanding."

If Mr. Dallek was experiencing frustration at the grays' reticence, he didn't show it, but I, on the other hand, or the part of my consciousness sitting in the recliner, felt as if it was continually trying to squeeze through a brick wall to procure answers. The aliens apparently shared information conditionally, with the terms being "if they allowed it."

Then the scene before my eyes suddenly changed.

"But...but now they're taking me into a room," I said, describing to Mr. Dallek what was happening in the strange world around me. "I see some aliens near an opening into a structure."

The gray being closest to me stepped up through a rounded doorframe, and with one hand clutching the left edge of the opening and one leg still on the ground, it slowly rotated its head and body and looked back at me. Somehow I knew I was supposed to follow.

I stopped for a moment to examine the creature. My eyes traced down the being's bone-thin leg, the one positioned through the opening and bent at the knee. The circumference of the thigh appeared to be nearly the same as the lower leg. *These beings are so strange*, I thought to myself.

"How are the little ones able to locate you?" Mr. Dallek asked.

I projected the question out into mental space, but no words came into my mind, only an image. "I see a gray, open area, like a tunnel. It seems to have something to do with this part of my head."

I reached up with my hand and placed it over a portion of my skull. In my mind's eye, the tunnel appeared within the left frontal lobe of my brain.

"Will the little ones tell you why they come for you in the night?" Mr. Dallek asked.

"I'm hearing something about purpose," I told him. "There is a purpose. I am their purpose. They learn from me, through me. It's as if they're saying that I'm their eyes and their ears. They need me to learn."

"Thank you," Mr. Dallek said. "Now tell the little ones, the gray beings, that they do not have your permission to use you in any way, to involve you in their purposes. It is inappropriate for another entity of consciousness to be present within your interdimensional space. You are here on your own spiritual path of learning. Therefore, the essence of your being and the path of your being should not be interfered with from this interdimension. They have no right, and you have your right of free will over this physical body vehicle—one spirit to one physical body."

While Mr. Dallek continued to emphasize his point, I struggled to make sense of the building confusion. I spent the next several seconds sorting through the jumble of thoughts and emotions that surfaced in response to Mr. Dallek's words. "I'm feeling resistance to the idea that they should leave me alone," I tried to explain. "It's a very strong feeling, though confusing."

A wall of resistance had suddenly divided my thoughts. Half of me was thinking: I want the aliens out of my life; I want to feel safe and secure in my home again. Yet the other half of my awareness voiced a sentiment that until that moment had never crossed my mind before: I know what this is about. The aliens *have* my permission.

I wondered if the short, gray beings had placed those thoughts into my head. Yet, that didn't seem likely. It was my impression that there really was a definite purpose to my involvement with the aliens, and that impression seemed to originate somewhere within my own mind. The aliens' thoughts had only confirmed it. And Mr. Dallek's insistence that the aliens were trespassing into my dimensional space and without my permission only heightened the pressure I felt from within to resist his suggestions.

Up to that point in the hypnosis session, it seemed that I was present in two separate worlds. Part of me was sitting in Mr. Dallek's office, while another part was standing with the aliens. During that time, I'd been searching for a comfortable cognitive position within that shifting double reality. Though my psyche was gradually adjusting, I could sense that my consciousness was trying to slip out of its cumbersome shell and step into a less restrictive environment. All it took was a mental nudge to effect the switch, and suddenly I was completely outside my physical body.

When my consciousness fully merged with the person standing in the aliens' realm, my awareness of self—the nature of my mind, the embodiment of all that I internally recognized as "me"—shifted in a peculiar way. I felt my psyche lose its gentle, feminine quality. And my humanness—as I experientially defined it—seemed to almost fade away. The human "me" was still there somewhere, but there was also another "me." That self was familiar, yet different at the same time, and it spoke through me with a mind of its own. My human thoughts were distinct from those of this other self, creating a duality of consciousness and sometimes an inner dialogue.

"What information do the little ones seek?" Mr. Dallek wanted to know.

"The experience of being human; what it is like to be in that form." The consciousness that I had merged with, the one standing with the aliens, had replied. "The female assists us in this, and it is important that she know who she is so she can move on to the next phase of the experiment."

"Thank you," said Mr. Dallek, and once again he emphasized that the aliens had no business entering my dimensional space, explaining that it was interfering with my life.

While Mr. Dallek was talking, I experienced the same peculiar emotional surge I had felt before. It could only be described as a feeling of arrogance, of haughtiness, and it was coming from the aliens' thoughts as they filtered down through my mind. It was as if the aliens were saying, "Who are you to tell us what we can and cannot do?" And somewhere in the midst of the assorted thoughts and emotions dancing around in my mind, my human awareness formed an opinion: These alien beings are not evil, but they are definitely icy, remote.

"Now I want you to slowly become aware of your surroundings," Mr. Dallek instructed. "As you become aware of your surroundings, look around and become aware if you're alone or if anyone is present with you."

Everywhere I looked, I saw gray—flat, boring gray, or shades thereof. The beings were gray. The walls around us were gray. The counter-like structures near the edge of the room were gray. There might have been something of interest on the counters, though, because I noticed a few black patches that stood out against the drab background.

From where I stood, I could see several aliens moving about in another room that was located straight ahead of me. These beings appeared to be completely engrossed in whatever they were doing on and near the counters. The only other aspect of the scene that grabbed my attention was the peculiar way the aliens standing near me had arranged themselves. They were standing in a row on my left, displaying a rather formal posture.

When I looked over toward the right side of the room, I immediately understood why the gray beings were positioned as they were. The aliens were facing what first appeared to be several floating balls of light.

I drew a deep breath, but before there was time to exhale, my human consciousness had been eternally transformed.

"I see little clouds of light, light beings, and I know them," I told Mr. Dallek. I was looking at white light, white vessels of light. They were shimmering, shifting, sentient forms. They were light beings, pure enchantment and my soul's bliss.

The light beings drifted toward me and encircled me in their radiance. The moment we touched, I shed my human identity, and any attachment I still had to my physical body completely dissolved away.

I merged with these wonderful creatures, our energies mingling, our forms twisting and twirling around each other in a manner no words could describe. We were bound together as one mind, one entity, souls touching souls, and composed of pure thought, pure energy, pure joy. It had been so long, so long that I had forgotten that this light was my natural state as a life form. It was my home, and the sparkling forms of light were my people, my Others. What happiness, what perfect peace, what rapture I knew in those moments of being inside my real self once again, communing with the universe and experiencing the pleasure and the power of my own light.

The frightened, constricted expression that had molded my face when the aliens first appeared was recast into a broad, placid smile. My fingers released their grip on the armrests of the recliner. In response, my hands automatically turned to expose my palms to the air, and I felt Mr. Dallek lightly grasping the edge of my right hand.

No single moment captured in my human memory had ever been as glorious. The only other time I came close to experiencing what I felt while merged with the light beings was during my youth, while staring up at the spaceships that had appeared over the farm. The presence of the ships had evoked feelings of recognition, elation, and hope. With the light beings' ethereal bodies wrapped around my own ethereal form, I experienced those feelings again. And in the same way it had happened when I telepathically spoke with the occupants inside the spaceships, my mind seemed to be filled with knowledge, though this time it was coming from the light beings.

Eventually, the light beings drifted away from me, returning to the place where I had first spotted them, which was only about an arm's reach away.

Mr. Dallek asked me some questions about the light beings, but it was nearly impossible to speak as a human. My mind wanted only to reach out toward the pulsating balls of light and to continue to merge with their energy. Even while standing inside my own ethereal form again, I could feel their omnipotent presence. Still, I tried to explain to Mr. Dallek that the light beings were telling me something. But I couldn't be more specific. My thoughts at that time were all clumped together. It was as if the light beings had downloaded volumes of information into my mind, but I couldn't retrieve the data in an intelligible form.

Within a couple of minutes, though, a concept did start to form. At first it was vague, but as I explored it in my mind, it solidified into a more complete awareness. It seemed that what the light beings were trying to tell me was that they knew about my involvement with the gray aliens. They were even radiating a sense of calm in regards to that involvement, as if they had given their blessing to the aliens' schemes.

I never explained this to Mr. Dallek, mainly because the idea didn't seem to fit. I obviously belonged with the light beings, not the aliens. I could easily relate to the light beings' soothing and nurturing light, but not to the aliens' flat emotional state and harsh, rigid psychic energy. The light beings were my family. The aliens were...well, they were simply alien.

Only minutes remained of the time established for the hypnosis session, so Mr. Dallek began to initiate my return from the depths of mind. First, he told me to bid farewell to the light beings. I responded to that request by immediately bursting into tears.

Panic gripped my soul. I knew that the light beings had to leave me, but I cried anyway. I couldn't help it. In that distant place in my mind, of aliens and light beings, I knew that I was about to be abandoned, abandoned again.

"How can I go on without them?" I asked, choking on the tears falling everywhere. "I want to go with them. How can I exist if they're not with me?"

The light beings were now floating away. They passed through the wall of the structure I was in, but I could still see them through it, and they appeared to be floating out into darkness, like the darkness of space. I watched in silence as the shimmering, shifting light bodies grew smaller, feeling a sense of longing that never entirely went away. I desperately wanted to follow them, my Others, my home. If it had been in my power to leave the recliner, to leave the earth, to leave all that I had known as a human female, I would have done so in that moment. I would have departed.

But my desire to leave was put into perspective when I heard Mr. Dallek say, "It is not your time to leave." And as I watched the beautiful wisps of light gradually fade into the distance, he added, "They are always with you. They are always around you. You know that, don't you?"

Part of me did know it, but right then that knowledge didn't matter. It wasn't enough to console the breaking heart of an abandoned soul, or whatever I was. I just wanted to be with the light beings, to go with them. I could still feel their overwhelming love, which was their limitless power, and from the direction of the barely visible balls of light, I heard a message: We *are* always with you. Then, I said with my mind, "Good-bye. Good-bye, and please stay close."

Sending the aliens on their way was not a problem. No emotional attachment, no bond, existed between us. The cavalier gray beings who had been lined up like soldiers seemed anxious to depart anyway. I watched them scatter in different directions. Their attention was no longer focused on me, giving the impression that a chore had been completed and now it was time to go.

"Allow your mind to move in a direction here today that will bring these events to completion and move you to a place of inner peace and balance." Mr. Dallek seemed to be opening a cosmic door and enabling me to take one last flight during our time together. "Move to that place in your mind," he said. "Be there now."

I was not expecting to go anywhere. The weight and denseness of my physical form was becoming more evident by the moment, and my mind, though still relaxed and in an altered state of consciousness, was perceiving a thin layer of fatigue that was spreading over my physical form. I was physically and emotionally drained, and since I could not go home with my Others, it was time to go back to my human life.

But Mr. Dallek's words had evidently triggered an automatic response that had set my mind into motion. My receptive psyche was still dutifully following Mr. Dallek's instructions, sending my conscious essence along the edge of time, toward another unknown destination. In a matter of seconds, the inky void before my closed eyes dissolved into patches of visual images.

"It's dark here," I said, knowing that Mr. Dallek was waiting for a response. "I'm in a room, a small room. I'm not sure what this is, but there's something here. A table. No. It's a chair. I'm sitting."

The images around me were slow to take shape. I had no idea where I was, as nothing around me provided clues to my location. Even the chair I reported to be sitting in was not an ordinary chair. It had a back and a seat, but somehow I knew it was not designed for comfort. It felt stiff, more like a structural component within a larger design.

"Look down at your body," Mr. Dallek directed, "and as you observe the body, describe what you see."

"Oh, what...what is this? My legs...my legs aren't like.... They're gray and wrinkled. They're like...they're like the aliens' legs. I look like one of those gray beings." I was expecting to see a human body, but the body that contained my consciousness held no resemblance to that familiar form. What I was looking at was an alien's body.

When the initial shock of seeing myself as an alien subsided, a numbing awareness took hold: The alien creatures have been abducting me because they know me; I'm part of them, and they recognize that part when we're together. Then, my mind leaped away from its own cognition, and I decided to keep my thoughts to myself.

Mr. Dallek asked me to comment on what I was experiencing, so I forced myself to step back into the scene and into the gray, skinny body to explore its sensations and its mind. Nothing came forth into my consciousness other than a stark emptiness, as if the alien wasn't thinking at all. The eyes I stared through looked around the dimly lit gray space, but observed only bare ceilings and walls. It seemed to me that I was just resting in the chair, or waiting for something.

I looked down at my bone-thin legs one more time, and then a rush of recognition passed through me. For a moment, it seemed that some part of me knew that body well.

Mr. Dallek slowly brought me back into my physical body. "One. Gently, easily, and calmly coming to a full waking state of awareness. The very moment your feet touch the ground, you will have the ability to release from your mind anything that is not appropriate in coming into consciousness here today. Subconscious mind is directed to only bring that which is appropriate into full waking consciousness for this person's benefit. Coming up. Two. Three. Four. Deep breath in. Eyes open. Fully aware. Fully awake in this time and place."

I opened my eyes and squinted, trying to adjust to the sudden burst of light. I glanced over at Mr. Dallek and shook my head back and forth to communicate my amazement at what had just transpired. When he released the footrest and my feet touched the ground, I leaned forward and dropped my face into my hands. The surface of my cheeks felt tight where spent tears had dried, leaving a salty residue, and then I remembered the many times I had cried during the session. I made a comment about it, intending to communicate my embarrassment.

Mr. Dallek assured me that there was no need to apologize for my tears. He said that hypnosis often released strong emotions. He was very supportive. And just before I moved off the recliner, Mr. Dallek said one more thing. He reminded me that the aliens could only interact with me if I allowed that to happen.

The concept of free will, and its recognition by other life forms, had never occurred to me before, though it made perfect sense. The alien beings I had crossed paths with over the years obviously possessed intelligence. They should at least be able to understand the concept of free will. But, if they did, why were they abducting humans? The aliens had to know by now that we didn't like it. And even if they had permission to abduct me, did that mean they had every abductees' permission?

I walked out of Mr. Dallek's office with a lot of questions on my mind, and in the days and weeks that followed, I reviewed everything that had taken place during the session. The events that I had participated in seemed so incredibly real, and there was no denying that the emotions I exhibited during the hypnosis session were genuine emotions. But what did it all mean?

I thought about the moment when the group of alien beings had surrounded me. Their sudden appearance had taken me by surprise. I was not even thinking about aliens prior to that moment, nor did Mr. Dallek ever prompt me to go looking for aliens. I wondered why I perceived that event as though it was occurring in the present, as if a part of my consciousness had been lifted into another dimension. I truly felt as though I were standing somewhere else, and during the entire time I stood with the light beings, I was barely aware that my physical body was sitting in Mr. Dallek's office.

And what about the light beings? How did I know undeniably that I was one of them, part of them? Why did I call them "my Others?" We came together as a group so naturally, sharing our conscious energies, and the ecstasy I experienced when I merged with these beings was positively transforming. But who were these beings? Were light beings a representation of the human soul—an extension of spirit, the higher self? Or were they a unique life form?

Question after question spun around in my mind, and though many issues were left unanswered, the hypnosis session did make one thing clear: My relationship with aliens was much more complicated than I had originally thought, and my wish to end my association with these strange creatures was never an option.

I thought about all the odd curiosities I had collected since childhood: spaceships in the sky, encounters with unknown life forms, unexplained electrical disturbances, the strong feeling of connection I sometimes felt during my alien-related "dreams." My strange memories now only deepened the mystery around my relationship with alien beings.

Were aliens really using me as their eyes and ears to learn about the experience of being human? Were they monitoring me, or was some part of me, part of them? After all, I had seen myself in a gray alien's body during my hypnosis session. Had I remembered that image from a previous lifetime, or was I actually an alien now, in a human body?

Just weeks after my hypnosis session, I had a profound dream that may have been intended to answer my questions. The dream took place in a room that appeared to be a cocktail lounge. Small bistro tables were scattered around the establishment. I was sitting at one of the tables, talking with two dark-haired men who appeared to be in their late twenties, maybe early thirties. I could not remember what we were talking about when I recalled the dream the next morning, but I knew our conversation had been light and friendly because we were sometimes laughing. The sunny mood at the table, however, quickly clouded over when one of the men looked straight at me and asked, "Are you an alien?"

The directness of the question and the man's demeanor took me by surprise. I immediately felt afraid. Both of the men were glaring at me, and I knew they were expecting a response. But I didn't know what to say. I didn't know the answer to the question.

In the midst of this exchange, a man who was sitting next to our table—an older man, probably in his fifties—swung around in his chair. In a calm, authoritative voice, he said to us "She is *of* an alien." The emphasis on the "of" was unmistakable. The man actually hung on that word for a couple of seconds.

It was just a dream, of course, but over the years my dreams had proven their reliability as teaching devices. The dream seemed to be telling me that only a part of me was alien. Maybe I shared a part of myself with something that was of alien origin.

During the first week in May 1992, alien beings showed up at my Minneapolis residence for another visit.

It may not have been their intention to bring me out of sleep, but one of the unexpected visitors who had entered my bedroom slammed against the edge of my bed. Whether a clumsy mistake or an intentional maneuver, it rocked the bed so forcefully that the sudden movement roused me from sleep. In the next instant, I knew that a small entourage of alien life forms were standing around in my bedroom.

Whenever the aliens were near me, I sensed their presence in the room. It was that unique inner awareness, that silent introduction that always announced the aliens' arrival during my encounters, even in years past. Looking back through my memories, I could remember perceiving that awareness even before I knew who I was dealing with. Within seconds of moving out of sleep and into consciousness, my mind would be filled with thoughts assuring me that whoever was near my bed had the authority to be there, and the activity taking place in the room posed no threat.

That reaction, of course, was counter to how I behaved when a human being happened to wake me from sleep. Whenever that happened, I would explode into a fully awakened state by an instinctive sense of alarm. Within seconds, I would be sitting up in bed with a pounding heart, often lambasting whoever it was who woke me when I wasn't expecting it. On the other hand, whenever the aliens awakened me, I typically would say to myself, *Oh, they're here again; just go back to sleep; everything is all right.* Hardly the words of someone surprised by an actual intruder.

This new encounter elicited the same relaxed response to the aliens' sudden arrival. I curled up in a fetal position and said to myself, *Here we go again.* The thought came into my awareness with the kind of clarity that spoke of my long association with the creatures standing next to my bed, and the trace of annoyance lining my unspoken words indicated that I was not particularly pleased with the aliens' attentions.

But I was in for a surprise. Instead of lapsing into unconsciousness, which I usually did after acknowledging the aliens' presence, this time I remained completely awake, and totally, painfully, aware of my situation. During all the encounters remembered from the past, never had I experienced any physical pain in association with the aliens' visits. But whatever the aliens did to me during the early hours of that particular morning, it definitely hurt.

I felt as if I were being electrically shocked. The muscles running down my back responded by contracting in a manner that reminded me of an experience I once had at the hands of a chiropractor who had wired me for electrical muscle stimulation to manage a case of back strain. In his attempt to locate the threshold at which my back muscles would automatically contract, he sent an electrical current through them that registered as pain. Whatever the aliens were doing, it was definitely above my pain threshold, and as the pulsating waves of electricity coursed through my back, I wondered why my visitors were torturing me. There was nothing I could do about it, though, as I was no longer able to move.

After about five or six excruciating jolts, the aliens were gone. I looked at my bedside clock and noticed that about fifteen minutes had elapsed since the last time I had checked the hour. I had woken up briefly just before the aliens had entered my bedroom, and had checked the time.

The following morning, I sat on the edge of my bed, cursing the interlopers for subjecting me to such a strange and painful procedure. There was no residual pain or physical discomfort, only a twinge of anger at having to endure their unannounced and unexplained assault. What were they doing?

That painful close encounter was followed by a less intrusive visitation a couple of weeks later. I woke up during the night to find a person standing next to my bed. I tilted my head upward slightly to allow a better view and realized that I was looking at what appeared to be a human male in his early thirties. He had dark brown hair that was styled close to his head and a diminutive physique. I estimated that his height was probably under five feet. I also noticed that he was wearing black slacks made from a fabric that reminded me of polyester and a long-sleeved, black knit turtleneck—an unusual choice of clothing, I thought, for a warm spring night. The man was hovering over me and staring down at my face. He must have had a hand on the wall above the headboard because his body was listing to the side at such a sharp angle that otherwise he would have fallen.

I didn't yell or scream. Oddly, I didn't react at all. I just nestled my head back into my pillow, and seconds before I drifted off into unconsciousness, I managed one final thought, *Oh, there's a man next to my bed; I'll go back to sleep now.* For someone suffering from panic attacks, that behavior didn't make any sense. I should have been screaming at the top of my lungs.

My memories of the strange little man and the pain I endured during the earlier encounter rested quietly within my psyche for quite a long time. Though I clearly remembered both events and replayed my peculiar perceptions over and over again in my mind, thinking about them didn't create any noticeable anxiety within me. Since the hypnosis session, I had been sleeping comfortably and not waking up during the night, except for the two encounters. The absence of any anxiety prompted me to consider that perhaps the experience of facing the aliens while under hypnosis had cured my fear of the strange creatures.

Whatever was responsible for my newfound tranquility, after about three weeks of normal sleep, it stopped working. My peaceful nights totally vanished. It seemed as if my mind suddenly broke through a barrier walling off the emotions that I normally would have expressed in response to waking up and finding strangers in my bedroom. When those emotions finally surfaced, my nights were filled with renewed fear and hysteria.

My life turned into a battle zone again. It was me, alone in my house, against an unseen world. I did what I could to fortify my surroundings against the creatures who mysteriously appeared in the night. I locked my bedroom door. I slept with a night-light turned on. Sometimes I left the overhead light on—all 120 watts worth. I even spent a few nights at the homes of my friends, Rita and Michelle, just to get a few hours of uninterrupted sleep. But standing in the front of my mind was the realization that all the defenses in the world could not protect me from the alien beings and whoever else was walking through my walls.

When I finally reached the point of exhaustion, I made another phone call to Mr. Dallek.

On June 15, 1992, I was once again sitting in his leather recliner.

CHAPTER 6

A Covenant to Serve

ALL THE TINY MUSCLES, all the tiny nerves in and around your eyes are to become so relaxed that whenever I touch your hand go deeper, now. As you go deeper, you breathe into the body. As you breathe out, each out-breath will continue to double the relaxation in your mind as the sound of my voice circulates and mixes with each and every out-breath."

I was now familiar with the induction, and I knew Mr. Dallek's technique to initiate a hypnotic trance was an effective approach. I quickly released my mind from its earthly concerns and relaxed into the moment, allowing the sound of Mr. Dallek's voice to float my awareness into the past.

"As I count from ten down to one, each number will double the relaxation of your mind. The number five will take you a thousand times deeper, and the number one will double it again. All things, all thoughts, all feelings, all sensations will move you deeper here today. As you go deeper, you become aware. You breathe into the body and go deeper, now. Ten. Gently and easily moving deeper."

More than two months had passed since I first felt the deep physical and mental calm that I now knew hypnosis could produce. I had left Mr. Dallek's office after that initial session completely relaxed and feeling confident that I could face whatever the future had in store for me. I wasn't exactly sure what that might be; maybe more alien encounters, more unexplained phenomena. I only knew that I didn't want to experience the exasperating anxiety and endless sleepless nights anymore.

After my first hypnosis session, I was able to sleep like a baby, despite a return visit from the aliens and even after waking up to find a human-looking being standing next to my bed. The typical pattern of anxiety that had become almost a way of life had mysteriously disappeared. Its absence restored my confidence in my ability to live without fear, even with the aliens' continuing presence in my life.

For nearly a month, I easily went about my normal routine: spending time with my friends and family; concentrating on my work as an instructional designer; enjoying the springtime weather; meeting some new people; cruising the paths around the city lakes on my bike or in-line skates; traveling now and then. Basically, I was involving myself in the human experience. Wasn't that what a part of me was here to do on the planet anyway, experience a human life? Wasn't that what the aliens wanted from me, a piece of my humanity, to live vicariously through my eyes and my ears?

I often wondered why they didn't just let me live my life without any knowledge of their existence. Since my childhood, they had been leaving a trail of evidence in my dream-like encounters and in a few unexplained conscious experiences. Either the gray aliens were bungling their own program or they wanted me to know they existed.

"Continue moving yourself deeper until we can move to a level of working here today," Mr. Dallek instructed, "going deeper and deeper. And as you go deeper, there's a certain feeling, a certain situation that we need to have knowledge of, a certain expectancy, a certain waking up, a certain feeling about needing to have the light on to feel safe, the door closed, a certain feeling: I'll be safe when it's light; I'll be safe when it's light out; I'll be safe when it's light out, and I can sleep. Going deeper and deeper, and as you go deeper and deeper, each beat of your heart continues to move you a hundred times deeper, as the sound of my voice circulates and mixes with each and every out-breath. Always going deeper here today. Always moving deeper, going deeper, now."

That "certain waking up" Mr. Dallek referred to was the reason I was again sitting in his leather recliner. My insomnia had suddenly returned, and with a vengeance. I had become a human clock with my alarm set at precisely the same time of night when the aliens had last paid me a visit—the night they bumped into my bed and shocked me with what felt like several strong jolts of electricity. My internal alarm was set for shortly after 1:00 a.m. Once awake, I would stand guard and watch for unusual forms to take shape in the room. It was typically 4:00 a.m. before my internal sentry went off duty, finally allowing me to close my eyes and return to sleep.

Still, the hours between 1:00 a.m. and 4:00 a.m. seemed endless. Though the door to my bedroom was locked and a light was turned on, I knew that such precautions offered no security against the aliens' unrestricted mobility. These night creatures could move through solid walls. Locked doors had not prevented their visitations before. For three hours I would lie awake and stare into the night, listening to the rhythm of my anxious heart, while knowing that at any moment the little gray aliens could appear before my eyes.

"And that feeling, that awareness, growing stronger and stronger, more and more powerful, stronger and stronger. And we're going to move to a room of healing and knowledge. We're going to move down ten steps to profound relaxation. Each step will take you a thousand times deeper. At the number one step, the doorway will be open into this room of healing and knowledge."

After weeks of broken sleep and long nights spent waiting for the first light of dawn, the opportunity to just sit quietly and relax, to be calm inside my mind, felt like a trip to paradise. I allowed my entire body to drop into the recliner and settle itself wherever it desired. It wasn't long before the muscles around my eyes stopped vying for control and my mind went searching for other aspects of itself by way of an altered state of consciousness.

"As we move from the tenth step, deeper now, down to the ninth and the eighth, deeper now, to the seventh, sixth, fifth, going deeper, go deeper now, down to the fourth, the third, the second, all the way down to one. As you step through the doorway into this room of healing and knowledge, the colors of this room are perfect healing colors. And this room is sealed and sur-rounded in an energy of healing light, as is your body sealed in light and protection as we work here today, as I seal my body in light and protection. I seal us in light."

An image of the light beings drifted across my mind. I enjoyed thinking about my Others, the ones who overwhelmed me with happiness, peace, and love in the middle of my first hypnosis ses-sion. I had wanted so much to be with them, to leave with them. Yet, the light beings had left me with the impression that all was as it should be within my human world. Still, I couldn't help but wonder why my human experience had become so painful. Why was I again drowning in my fears? Was this all part of the next phase of the aliens' experiment?

"As you step into this room, in the very center of this room is a very comfortable place for you to lie down. A place that supports your body perfectly in every way. As you lie down, you go twice as deep. As you go deeper, you breathe into the body. As you breathe into the body, breathe out and go twice as deep, as each beat of your heart moves you a hundred times deeper, as all feelings, thoughts, and sensations continue to move you deeper. As you go deeper, you breathe into the body, and there's a certain feeling growing stronger and stronger, more and more powerful. Your awareness of that feeling, growing stronger and stronger, more and more powerful."

Mr. Dallek touched my chin, as he had done during the previous session, while inviting my subconscious mind to speak.

"What area of the body holds the energy that needs attention? Voice can speak free and clear."

"The mind," I said, allowing whatever seemed appropriate to come forth.

"Breathe into the mind. As you breathe into the mind, go deeper. As you breathe into the mind, your awareness grows stronger and stronger. And as you breathe into the mind, become aware of the color of the energy and give a report. What color is the energy as you breathe into the mind?"

"Yellow," I said, though the word had jumped out of my mouth before I had time to give the question any thought. I wondered why I would choose that color. But then I reminded myself not to judge my own responses. It was better to just sit back and listen to my inner voice speak its mind.

"Thank you," Mr. Dallek said, in the gracious manner he addressed my altered consciousness. "Breathe into the yellow. Energy of yellow, growing stronger and stronger in your awareness, more and more powerful. Stronger and stronger, more and more powerful, stronger and stronger. As you breathe into the yellow, the first word, thought, feeling, whatever pops into your mind."

"Safety."

"Say again."

"Safety," I said.

"Thank you. Energy of yellow—safety, safety, safety. Energy of yellow, growing stronger and stronger, stronger and stronger, safety, safety, safety. Now we're going to count from ten down to one, and we're going to move back in time along the pathways of this energy. As we move back along the pathways of this energy, the energy in your awareness will become stronger and stronger, more and more powerful. On the number one, we're going to be in the time and place a few minutes before this energy ever became a part of you. The portals of all time are open. All time is open and available to us. As I count from ten down to one, moving back, flowing back, moving back. Nine. Moving back, flowing back. Eight. Safety, safety, energy of yellow growing stronger and stronger, those feelings flowing out of your body. That feeling becoming so powerful, now. Moving back, flowing back, eight, seven, six, five, four, three, two, one. Be there now. Daytime or nighttime, indoors or outdoors? Look around."

"It's night," I said, making that assumption because it was dark wherever I was.

"Indoors or outdoors?"

"Indoors."

"And look down at your body. Look down at the feet and slowly begin moving up, becoming aware of what covers the body, how the body's dressed. Male or female?"

"Female."

"And look around. Is there anyone else in here? Take a look. Are you alone or are others here? This female, look around."

"I don't see anyone else," I said.

"Thank you. We're going to move up to that significant situation that has to do with this. Moving up. One. On the count of three, being at that significant situation, coming up. Two. Three. Be there now, and become aware of what takes place here, this female."

"I see this little girl that I've seen before. And, umm, she...actually, it's like sometimes inside, and sometimes I see outside, and when she's inside, she's alone. But when she's outside...there *they* are, those creatures."

The "outside" image I saw in my mind was of a small child. She could not have been much more than two years old, as the scuffed-up shoes she was wearing—the kind that tie up the front and are flat on the bottom—placed her near that age. She was wandering about in an open meadow, walking slowly and clumsily through the tall grass that reached past her shoulders. A steady breeze whipped the grass into circular patterns and caused the child's light colored, printed dress to billow out now and then and her thin, golden curls to straighten against her face. I was sure in my mind and in my heart that the little girl was a much younger version of me.

When I first saw the child, she was about four or five feet away. Then, after a few seconds, my point of view shifted and I was able to perceive the scene from the child's own eyes. I was looking up at a group of gray aliens.

"There they are," Mr. Dallek said. "There are those creatures. Take a look at them."

"They're taking my hand."

"And see where they take you."

I gasped, paused, then spoke in a whisper, "This is so strange."

I saw my own chubby little hand reach out and grab hold of a hand unlike any I had ever seen before. The contrast between my tiny white fingers and the gray flesh of the alien's hand cemented the image in my mind. The alien's remarkably long, tapered fingers clasped over my own. Then the creature walked me toward a small, gray metallic craft that sat in a clearing near the edge of some woods. The bottom of the structure was sitting up off the ground, and from my height of about two and a half feet, the closer I got to it, the more I had to look up to view it.

"See where they take you. Be aware of your feelings. Allow it to happen. Little girl, what are you feeling?"

"My little girl seems to be okay. She's just following along, and, umm, but she goes inside and is standing kind of in a spot that's not...really seems dark. It's like there's this blank when she's inside. And it's like she's not really aware, she's just there."

"Thank you. And when she's outside, these creatures take her or wish to lead her away somewhere. And see where these creatures wish to take her."

"I see her sitting on a bench," I offered. "She's really fine. She's just looking around."

"She doesn't seem to be too upset. Take a look and see."

"No," I said, confirming that the little girl was not frightened or upset.

"What do you think they want to do with her?"

"She doesn't know, but it's like I hear, umm, 'they just want to study her.'"

"They just want to study you?" he said.

"But she knows them," I added.

Then Mr. Dallek asked, "She knows them because she's met them before?"

"I think so, " I said. "A long time before then. Another time."

"Another lifetime before that lifetime."

"Yes."

"In fact, if you take a look inside the little girl, perhaps you may even discover that the energy of her being is one and the same as those that came to get her. Take a look and see. Look inside her and see if the essence of her being is one and the same as the creatures'. See if there's a similarity."

"Similar, yet different," I explained.

"Thank you. Now become aware of your feelings. Why are you upset about this?"

"It's...it's that I sense their energy, and it's...it's harsh, and it's uncomfortable."

"Very scientific, matter of fact, no love, no feeling."

I tried to explain exactly what I was feeling. "It's like, umm, it's like knowing them, about them, seeing. It's that knowing of them isn't the problem, it's feeling them that's, umm, difficult and uncomfortable."

"Feeling their presence?" Mr. Dallek asked.

"Yes."

"Thank you."

"And seeing them," I added. "But the little girl is not afraid."

"And yet you sense an experience. Your concern is for her. You have insight where she doesn't, or perhaps her senses aren't tuned in to needing to be afraid."

"She's not," I confirmed.

"Now become aware. We're going to move back in time to the very first time you encountered the little ones that come. Moving back to the very first time you ever encountered the little ones that come. Moving back, flowing back, ten, nine, eight, to the very first time you ever experienced the little ones coming, seven, six, five, four, three, two, one. Be there now. Daytime or nighttime, indoors or outdoors?"

"It's the same scene," I said. I was again observing the little girl that I believed to be me playing in a field of long grass.

"Now look down at your physical body and become aware. Is your physical body large or small? And what covers your physical body?"

"Really small. Little shoes. I shouldn't be by myself where I am. Maybe two years old."

"And look around and become aware of what happens next, the very first time."

"Hmm. I'm sitting up, and they're looking at me."

"And did they communicate with you in any way? See if there are thoughts moving back and forth between you. Child, are you afraid of these things you're seeing?"

"No, curious."

"Then become aware of what happens next."

"I just see them lift, lifting the little girl off of this chair, kind of like a platform that she's sitting on, and she's just kind of wandering around."

"See where they took her."

"I get the sense they want to show her something."

"And if you take a look at their size, is their size about the same size as she is?"

"No, she's very small," I explained. "They're...they have to look down to see her."

"Okay. As she's looking up at them, become aware. Describe how they appear to her."

"They look odd," I said, "because they have such skinny arms and legs."

"And become aware of the color of their bodies."

"It's all the same color. They're all kind of mottled gray."

"Thank you."

I continued to inspect the gray figures in front of me, intrigued by the way their bone-thin appendages performed. "When they move, they are very lanky," I reported. "Their movements are lanky."

"And see what happens next."

"It seems like someone picks her up, but I can't tell. It doesn't seem like the creatures pick her up."

"Bodies being lifted? See where the body moves to next."

"I just feel like I'm back out in that field in that long grass. It's almost as tall as I am."

"Go ahead and be at the field," Mr. Dallek instructed. "Become aware of what happens next."

A black and white dog suddenly came into view, and I followed it out of the field. I realized then that I was only a short distance from my parents' house. That didn't make sense to me, though, because the field I walked out of was not the same place where I had first observed the little girl. It seemed as if I had been in two separate places.

"There's a dog that comes, and I think it's my father. Hmm."

I saw my father coming toward me from across the yard, as if he had just come out of the house.

"And see what happens next," Mr. Dallek instructed.

"I'm just looking at my father. He looks so young." A giggle slipped out while I studied the youthful image of my dad. I rarely ever saw him outdoors without a cap on his head, but this image showed him without one. I felt a surge of tender emotion as I watched my father draw near.

"And become aware if there is surprise in finding you here."

"Somewhat," I offered. "He's just leading me out of there."

My attention shifted from my father to the black and white dog, and for a moment, I lost myself in the toddler's perceptions. "There's a dog. He's almost as tall as I am."

"And now it's time to become aware of what took place between being lifted up and between being in the field. All blocks cleared now."

"It's that feeling of being in darkness, surrounded in darkness," I said. "It's the same thought [as] when I was trying to see [how I had gotten to the field where I encountered the gray creatures]. I feel this sort of void, this darkness all around."

"That darkness, that void, become aware of that darkness, that void. That darkness, that void, is to keep you from moving into an understanding of what happened. But you are older now, and your adult intelligence has already made contact with the fact that they [aliens] exist. Therefore, anything that took place is now appropriate to come into your consciousness, anything that took place. I wish you to step into the darkness and step through to the other side and see what's there."

"I'm hearing in my mind these words that say that they want me back."

"Say that again."

"They want me back."

"Say it again."

"They want me back," I repeated.

"Now think it over and over in your mind."

"They want me back with them to complete the studies." I paused for several seconds, then said, "A part of me is asking them why."

"Go ahead. Listen to their response."

"I just hear, 'You'll understand later.' I'm saying, That's not good enough; I need to know." I was carrying on a dialogue with what seemed like a pool of alien minds, and their collective thoughts were converging into a single communication. The aliens came back again with a response, saying, "It's not your time to know."

"Now do the next best thing," said Mr. Dallek. "Your experiment with me is over for I have a will and a choice of my own. You have no right to be in my space. You have no right to come to me during that period when I am vulnerable and open in my dream state. You have no right. I do have the choice of free will, and that is my right. I choose not to be a part of your experiment. I choose for you to release all openings, all communication lines, all implants, all openings."

"I'm hearing, 'She knew the consequences,' as weird as that sounds," I told Mr. Dallek.

"Then I present to the female here: female, was there an agreement between you in some way that was of mutual benefit between you?"

Mr. Dallek's question surprised me. It put into words a concept that had been forming in my consciousness ever since the first hypnosis session. But I had not discussed my thoughts about it with Mr. Dallek, nor had I mentioned the word "agreement" to him.

"I think there must have been," I said. "I feel this, this internal resistance to the thought about, umm, that they have to go away."

Mr. Dallek chose to address the aliens directly. "Is the essence of her being one and the same as the energy and the essence of your being?"

"No, it's similar. She's been altered," I said, though my words were not coming from my awareness. I could sense another mind standing close to my own, and the words were definitely transmissions from an alien consciousness. I spoke them, but my mind, my individual consciousness, was centered elsewhere.

Actually, I was still wondering about the agreement, wondering what that was all about.

Apparently, Mr. Dallek was curious about that, too. He probed for more information, "And so she has been altered in order to accommodate physical human form. Is this correct?"

"Yes." Again a response came forth, but not from me. It came from someone speaking through me.

"So basically the experiment here is the implant of the essence of your type of being or spiritual essence or nature of being into physical form to see what develops. Is this correct?"

"Partly."

"Thank you."

In the midst of the dialogue between Mr. Dallek and the alien consciousness speaking through me, I finally understood why I was resisting the idea that my involvement in the aliens' experiment come to an end. Whoever was talking with Mr. Dallek was a part of me. That particular consciousness existed within the whole of my psyche, and somehow I knew that we could not be separated. It was through the alien's awareness, this other consciousness, that the alien beings were able to learn about humans. I could be their eyes and their ears, but the alien consciousness was the conduit. She translated my life experience into a language that those of her kind could understand. That was part of the experiment.

Flashes of insight continued to burst forth, along with images that told a bizarre story. During my first hypnosis session, there had been a moment when I saw myself as an alien life form with skinny, gray legs. I now understood that those legs had once belonged to the alien consciousness that shared my physical body. It was also this alien consciousness that had recognized the squadron of spaceships seen on two separate occasions when I was still a young girl. The dichotomous switch between fear and overwhelming joy that occurred during the encounter was caused when my human consciousness was pushed aside and the alien consciousness came forward into my awareness. The flood of knowledge that filled my mind during that event was actually the contents of another consciousness rushing into the fore.

I had two consciousnesses, two separate minds, two distinct psyches—a human self and an alien self. That duality of awareness explained why I could be calmly aware of the aliens' presence during an encounter and absolutely terrified while remembering it later on. My alien self knew that it was perfectly acceptable for alien life forms to be walking around in my house.

Once convinced that my involvement in the aliens' activities was part of an agreement, Mr. Dallek directed his questions toward broadening our understanding of its purpose.

"Let's move back in time to the moment you agreed to this task. Moving back, moving back in time to a time and place where there was a request or perhaps a discussion that has to do with your partaking of this plan and the need for this experiment. Moving back, ten, nine, eight, seven, six, five, four, to that time and place, three, two, one. Be there now."

"I'm seeing the same scene I saw before, where the gray beings are all lined up on the left and the light beings are on the right, and I'm standing somewhere back from that but, there's, there is some kind of communication about my role in this." I was referring to the events that took place during my first hypnosis session after the light beings appeared.

"If we combine the energies of that which you are and that which we are...."

"Humans?" I asked, wanting clarification, but in the process I interrupted Mr. Dallek's thought.

"Um-hmm, or light beings and scientific gray. See if there is some alliance or some way to try and connect the two. Hear what your role is in this."

"Something about my understanding will allow me to cope with the realities of my being who I am."

"Now move back to a time in the reality when you see exactly who you are. Move back to that reality, or if you've experienced this in a way to help you cope, then observe yourself for who you are."

"I'm very light," I told Mr. Dallek. "Whatever this is, it's very peaceful, very powerful, and comfortable and good."

"Absorb yourself in those feelings and understandings."

"I can feel other energy, other people, other minds."

"Open a channel to those energies—collective mind consciousness. Those are the higher beings, those are the light beings, those are the higher ones who collect the energy of the mind or have collective consciousness into peace and to oneness and to wholeness."

"They tell me I have no reason to be afraid; there is a wholeness, that we are one. They say I should reach out to them more often."

"Ask if they are aware of your agreement in any way to the grays."

"They're saying, 'You chose to step into their light to discover, to discover yourself.'"

"Thank you. And ask them, as you stepped into their light, is it one and the same light as the light that the human form shares?"

"No, their light is different," I pointed out. "Something about purpose. Their purpose...well defined. Humans have no purpose?" That communication was not coming from the light beings. I was receiving thoughts from the collective alien consciousness. I merely reported what I heard, but my shock at the aliens' impertinent attitude toward humans turned their comment into a question.

"They're so haughty," I said to Mr. Dallek, offering him my opinion. "They're just so stubborn. There's a part of me that's just asking them, 'Why me?' and 'Why isn't this more pleasant if I chose this?'"

"If you are in perfection and in completion and in harmony, if you chose to recognize yourself, sometimes you place yourself in vehicles or places and circumstances that create the difference of sensing and knowing and feeling. The possibility is that you are now recognizing that you chose this, and the physical embodiment that has to do with fears, unpleasantness, needs to connect with that peace and that collective consciousness to know that you have chosen this mission, chosen this task, that you have nothing to be afraid of.

"And if there was an agreement to move towards completion with the grays for some greater purpose for that of the collective consciousness or the higher light beings' consciousness, if you had chosen to do a job, and you have forgotten the mission, and you were simply caught in a moment of fear in between not understanding, when things become clear and knowledge flows, then you can be satisfied in a direction things are going.

"For you have always had the choice of being in control here. You have always had the choice to close the door and the ability to close the door. For no one is a slave to another, another's will, not as long as you have free will, and you have free will. You do not need me to speak for you or to direct you. You have free will. And in so doing, you have the right to terminate.

"But it is important, perhaps, to gain further insight so that we get the full picture, for the importance of this circumstance may be of such magnitude, and there may be others that are relying upon you in this mission in some way. So you may be able to acknowledge that this is happening, yet stay in a balanced end state where you can live out this life and be who you are.

"But also, this other mission is being worked on. I ask the higher ones here to move this forward to completion so that she become aware of what the completed project or outcome may be."

I then said to Mr. Dallek, "The light beings are saying something that I can only interpret as: I'm like a satellite. That word 'satellite' comes to me, radiating light as the sun. Balance...keeping energy in balance. Simply that."

"And asked if there is anything you need to fear, and the answer was no. Ask if the grays have permission to work with you."

"Yes," I said.

"And in so doing, can it be done in such a way that it would not intrude into your awareness or consciousness or senses so that you could move forward and live in this physical body in peace without knowledge of their intrusion."

"Hmm. I get the sense that the light beings have recognized that's where they've [the grays] failed to maintain their side of the agreement."

"Fully conscious of the aspect of being in this body is that you're not supposed to be aware of any of this."

"That's right," I said.

"So there's been a breach on both sides."

"They [the collective alien consciousness] say it's me, that I'm partly the cause because of who I am. I'm able to..."

"Break through your own barriers."

"...see them." I continued. "That's part of my confusion: the conflict between recognition and the fear attached to that and my own higher awareness."

"It's kind of like being in two places at once," Mr. Dallek said. "You have knowledge and understanding of all that is taking place, yet when it presents itself to you, there is a momentary gap that allows you the confusion of not being able to understand what is going on here. It is kind of like being in two places at once. Being in a place where you're not supposed to understand, yet you see. Yet you see, and you also understand.

"So, therefore, if you have processed that awareness, then you can also move your mind to a place where you can filter out any awareness, unless it is one that would cause imminent danger or harm. If this is a part of something that's going on, um, it's okay.

It's okay to allow yourself to move into deep sleeps, and allow your agreement or your arrangement to continue, if that is your desire or if that is what is appropriate. Ask the light beings if it is appropriate to continue here."

"Something about my curiosity, a door has opened," I said, trying to interpret the information coming into my mind, "and my own curiosity is keeping it open."

"Well, in other words, if you're part of an experiment where you're not supposed to be aware of it, and a door was opened through your gift of insight because of who you are, and now you have not been given the answer. For if you were given the answer, then the experiment would not be valid. So you have a set of circumstances here that is kind of a Catch-22, which means, aah: 'I'm aware of all that's taking place, yet I choose not to be aware, because that is part of what I chose to experience in order to complete this mission' and, on the other hand, 'I kind of want to be aware of these things when they come to visit and play, and see what they're doing, and see what they're up to'...Is this correct?"

"Um-hmm."

"And then the energy in the event brings you to waking consciousness and you're left with this anxiety that little creatures are walking around in here, taking the little girl somewhere. That is the image you've been holding on to, and something did take place between the first encounter. Perhaps you were taken someplace, and the circumstance was set up, an experiment was set up."

"That happened before I was born," I said.

"Thank you. So, as a light being, you chose to come into physical embodiment and with an agreement."

"Yes," I said.

"With the grays. Thank you. Now move your mind to a place where you can work this to a place where you can benefit all parties here. Simply allow yourself to move into a deeper state of sleep that will last and be healing and restful to you."

The tape recorder clicked off, producing a loud, distracting noise that jolted my mind back into the physical reality around me.

While resetting the tape recorder, Mr. Dallek suggested that I mentally switch off my awareness during my encounters "at the times that would be appropriate for completion."

"That would work," I said. "I feel resistance inside myself. It's like I want to see and to know. There's a part of me that says, 'I want to be able to look at their faces,' because for some reason that's the part that's so difficult."

"Then move your mind to the place and look at their faces and confront them and keep looking at them until any fear, any mis-understanding, is moved aside, for you are here to encounter and learn and to move yourself beyond those feelings."

"I can't see them [the aliens' faces]. I get this feeling that they're blocking that. I'm hearing something about...part of the experiment is kind of a conditioning of that visual experience. Part of the study is the fear of seeing them, human beings seeing them. I ask them, 'Why?' and I hear, 'Because it will eventually happen.' They need to know how we process that experience. I can see their bodies distinctly. I can...I can see their arms and their legs, but as soon as I work my mind's eye up to their neck, it becomes shrouded."

"Because they do not want the intelligence of your person to process that which the experiment is about. They wish to come to you in complete surprise and to get the clear path of energy of that expression of fear as it is presented to you. Yet the girl sat with them unafraid, almost unaware of their presence, as if they weren't there, but you could see them. So from her viewpoint, they may not have been there at all. She may have just been sit-ting on that bench, or being perhaps led by some other illusion that created itself in a way that would not cause her difficulty.

"You see, sometimes things can be presented to you in a form that is not harmful or fearful. In fact, the technique is used very often when the human spirit leaves the physical body. It is accommodated with what it expects in the heaven: to go over the grassy knoll; to move across the water. Things in the other dimensional plane are quite different, and therefore the human spirit needs to be acclimated in a way that allows itself to see what it needs to see in order to be comfortable with the process.

"Similarly, this energy of fear that something's different—something that goes beyond our belief system—is very much appropriate. But that is what makes us human.

"Also, there are other entities and energies at work here, for if we look at the spiritual essence of the human's body—physical and spiritual—we recognize that there can be spiritual beings outside of the physical body that are still in presence...there are other kinds of beings, intelligences of consciousness, besides just the grays.

"So perhaps this meeting between the grays and the light beings has a greater significance on a universal scale, not just for the human, for there are many intelligences and many forms throughout the many dimensional planes and other universal planes here. There are many that chose to come into physical embodiment to partake of this task and to prepare mankind for the transformation, the transition that's taking place. It is not just the arrival of some extraterrestrial, for this is of greater significance, for you must realize yourself that in this other dimensional plane there are also barriers that can be crossed into the spirit world, for the grays have invaded and basically made contact with the spirit of the being, its essence of the soul.

"So what we're looking at is really the opening of the humans' consciousness into areas that they have been unable to see themselves before. For, in fact, are we not doing this now? In fact, you were doing it now."

"Yes," I said, agreeing with Mr. Dallek.

"So the things that go bump in the night, the things that come out of the woodwork, that simply shift from one dimension to another, they've been able to do that for quite a long time, as have many other beings or entities or energies or spiritual essences or other dimensional knowledge. Seems like we're the last ones to know. So basically, we do not wish to overwhelm the human consciousness or psyche unless it is ready and prepared.

"It's kind of like, how do we help the humans develop the ability in such a way that all that seems so foreign, so unbelievably—perhaps in their judgment—grotesque or unusual, can be presented to us in such a way that we can neutralize the negative effect, that we can present in such a way the inner peace and harmony of the light being that is in such oneness and wholeness? It sees no need to fear. It sees no need to differentiate. It senses in a different way. It feels in a different way. There's just a knowingness, and there's also the collectiveness of the minds that allows it to process in a whole different way.

"But each human is a separate entity, kind of locked into itself, locked into a process, yet very much still not aware of the greater whole. The transformation seems to be unlocking the consciousness into the greater whole.

"Now, to take it upon this one female here in the chair...for there are many. You are not the only one. There are many, many others partaking in many different kinds of experiments, and you are definitely loved and supported by those of your kind. Then, we move our minds back to the simplicity of, How do I get a good night's sleep, as I have been in a physical body? And allow that answer to come to you now."

"'Understand. Seek understanding in the light,'" I said, repeating what was coming into my mind. "Something about...'as in the light in your room.'"

"Thank you. Nothing else need be said. For some reason you feel that you can keep the bogeyman away when there is light, and when you close the physical door, it protects you and keeps you safe in your room. The feeling of safety allows the person to continue through a full night's sleep in peace and harmony. As you look into the light, you've recognized that the energy of light is always with you and always surrounds you, that you are in peace or in completion. There is no need to fear or to be awakened for you are protected in all ways, and all is as it should be.

"See the light surround your body now, and see yourself lying down, getting ready to go to sleep. Surround yourself in light, protect yourself in light. Feel the warmth and comfort of those other light beings above you, loving you, protecting you, and watching over you. We are here with you, and you are not alone. We are aware of all that takes place for you. Trust us. You can release yourself into good hands and drift off into a deep and pleasant sleep and rest. We watch over you, we protect you, and we are aware of all that you need. As you drift into sleep, we are here, we are love. You are not alone. I surround myself with that light and I see myself drifting off into a deep, deep, restful, healing sleep. I awaken at a certain time that's appropriate to allow me to move through my work day, my creative day, in this human body, doing the things that I need to do in this physical world. I rest deeply in deep, healing, restful sleep, and my physical body awakens refreshed, energized and ready.

"But see the cocoon of light energy and warmth surrounding you, filling the darkest room with light, and see the door closed in such a way that it will remain closed. But only those who have the permission—they don't even have to open the door, they just simply move through it, and the door can remain closed, safe, and secure—only those who have permission as prearranged or agreed can move through the door, for I will not open the door. It only has access to those who know. The door shall remain closed so that there are no other energies or entities that can enter in through the door. This allows me to feel safe. This allows me to know that it's been prearranged that the light beings will observe in my best interest, and those that need access for this particular experiment may do so without my conscious knowledge. I release my well-being to those of the light, as I am one, and if this is appropriate, then we will solve the issues here today. You now have permission to drift off into a deep, healing sleep. You also have permission, as is appropriate in some future time, to allow this knowledge of what is taking place here to merge into your consciousness and to gain greater benefit.

"For you are, as I am, performing certain tasks and roles that seem to be beyond our own conscious awareness. I would like very much to know why I am doing what I am doing, and what my purpose is here. But it is inappropriate for me to have the knowledge unfolded to me, for I have to discover it for myself and find that meaning, that truth, at an appropriate time. I just simply have to have faith that all is as it should be, and part of the process is learning and sharing and opening to a greater good and whole.

"See yourself drifting off into that deep sleep, deep, restful sleep, all night. The body resting, relaxing, and perhaps drifting off to very pleasant, pleasant dreams, pleasant places, pleasant experiences, healing thoughts, and lock that into your mind now."

Mr. Dallek snapped his fingers to set the suggestion into my mind. Then he said, "Any time you lie down on your bed for purposes of sleep, the moment your head hits the pillow, you're going to feel a very deep need to drift off into a deep, restful sleep. Whenever your head hits the pillow, you're going to feel a great need to drift off into a deep, restful, healing sleep, where wonderful, beautiful, wonderful, beautiful places, experiences, can be found, and perhaps some problem solving or things that pertain to our daily tasks in this world, moving towards positive outcomes and benefits. The moment your head hits the pillow, you're to drift off into a deep, restful sleep, just like that." Mr. Dallek snapped his fingers a second time.

"One. Gently, easily, and calmly coming to a full waking state of awareness. The very moment your feet touch the ground, you will have the ability to release from your mind anything that is not appropriate in coming into consciousness here today. Subconscious mind is directed to only bring that which is appropriate into full waking consciousness for this person's benefit. Coming up, two, three, four. Deep breath in. Eyes open. Fully aware, fully awake in this time and place."

Acclimating to my human world required both a physical and an emotional adjustment. For more than an hour, I had been free of the denseness, the confinement, and the limited potential that being in a human body imposed on my consciousness. Forced to accept those restrictions again, I reluctantly returned to my physical form.

I remained in Mr. Dallek's leather recliner for several more minutes. Aside from having to adjust to the bright light in the room, I needed time to make the awkward transition between altered consciousness and normal consciousness and between telepathic communication with a multitude of dimensional beings and verbal communication with Mr. Dallek. I didn't know what to say to him during those few minutes. So many strange things occurred during my hypnosis session that I could only sit in the recliner and look surprised, which I was.

This second session revealed more bits of bizarre information. Apparently, as a light being, I had come into physical form with an alien consciousness to enable the gray aliens to study the human condition. The aliens hadn't targeted me out of the millions of humans on the planet for contact, my life as a human female was part of a well-designed plan. And I had agreed to participate in that plan while existing in another dimension of reality, prior to being born. I was never a target of what I had thought were the aliens' threatening machinations. In actuality, I was a willing participant in their schemes. I had just forgotten that I had given my consent.

The only question that remained was whether or not my awareness of the alien beings and my knowledge of their activities was supposed to surface at this time in my life. Had I broken through the barriers ahead of schedule, only to suffer the consequences in the form of fear? But, from the knowledge gained during my hypnosis session, even my fear had a part to play in the gray beings' experiment. The aliens wanted to know how a human processed the experience of seeing them. I could only hope that they had collected enough data.

If the aliens were monitoring my emotional response to their movements in and out of my conscious world, they were getting a solid performance, one that I believed was representative of the human population. Learning to accept the existence of alien beings had been a lengthy and agonizing process. It began with disbelief, anxiety, denial, fear, partial acceptance, continued fear, concern for my personal safety, tears, anger, confusion, and exploding paradigms. The process ended with new realities, wonder, awe, demand for respect, and finally an awareness that explained my personal involvement. Such were the elements within the spectrum of a human's experience in the face of alien contact. For me, that experience had become the most difficult challenge of my human life.

If the aliens were paying attention to what was happening to me emotionally, intellectually, and spiritually, they would have learned a valuable lesson: Humans are survivors; we learn; we grow; we change, sometimes for the worse, but mostly for the better. It was not always obvious to me, but my experiences with aliens were teaching me important lessons about myself and about the universe around me. Because of the disbelief, denial, and fear that started my education, I was changing for the better.

Perhaps that was the direction the aliens were pushing me all along: deep into the core of my psyche and my soul, where secrets of the dimensional universe awaited to be discovered. In order to understand the aliens' unique world and to recognize my own soul and my dimensional roots, it was critical that I look there first. That understanding would have to be firm before I could be introduced to the alien consciousness who was observing my human life while sharing my existence. And only then could I fully grasp the purpose underlying my human life.

When I left Mr. Dallek's office on that day in June 1992, I walked down the hall with a bent smile on my face. I was thinking about the irony attached to the outcome of my strategy to end my relationship with aliens, and it humored me. Only months before, I had announced that I was ready to go to war with my alien intruders. Then, almost in the same breath, I discovered that the gray beings and I were on the same side—whatever side that was on and in whatever dimension. Not only had I confirmed the existence of alien beings in my life, but I reaffirmed my vow to serve the covenant I had made with them long ago, with the light beings as my witness and in the name of my dimensional soul.

CHAPTER 7

A Mind in Metamorphosis

DURING THE DAYS AND WEEKS that followed my hypnosis sessions with Gary Dallek, memory-images of the light beings frequently drifted into view. Whenever the radiant, pulsing forms of light appeared again in my mind's eye, I readily slipped into an altered state of consciousness, not distantly removed from the present—which was my experience during hypnosis—but distant enough to attain what I regarded as a heightened sense of awareness.

While in that meditative state, powerful emotion would well up inside me and an automatic smile would sweep across my face. I discovered that merely thinking about the light beings and visualizing their brilliant white forms was in itself a natural tonic. Their image soothed and nurtured my human psyche, liberating me from the physical world, while enlivening my soul.

Seeing the ethereal beings again in my mind transported my waking consciousness to a different level, another realm. There I would stand in a white pool of light that was both magical and transforming.

During the weeks following my hypnosis sessions, I felt as if I was undergoing an extraordinary change. It seemed that luxuriating in the light beings' radiance was triggering a spiritual awakening. It was like a metamorphosis of consciousness that resulted in the molting of my humanness and the rebirth of my soul. Every time I recalled the sweet memory of seeing myself, my true essence, in the light beings' ethereal glow, it was as if broad, sweeping wings suddenly unfolded, allowing my soul to take flight.

That poignant moment when I recognized my spiritual body in the shimmering, shifting balls of light was the most profound experience of my human lifetime. It revealed volumes of cosmic history in a few short seconds, a history reminding me of my heritage, reminding me that I had another home and another identity, a spiritual identity represented by my soul. It was my infinite life force. While standing in the presence of aliens in a dimension far beyond the physical boundaries of earth, I remembered what it felt like to leave my physical body and to stand inside my soul once again. When the light beings encircled me in their conscious light, I remembered what it felt like to instantly melt into gold.

Though mind-boggling against the backdrop of my human self-image, the unexpected, yet glorious encounter with the beings of light reminded me that I was a light being, a sentient form with consciousness, capable of emotional thought, but without the physical limitations inherent to a corporeal body. My natural ethereal form carried the essence of my individual consciousness, yet could shine through time and dimensional space, radiating the energy of my thoughts far out into the universe. As a light being, my consciousness could instantly merge with another mind, as well as hold council with an entire collection of psyches. I discovered that I possessed that capability while wrapped in the light beings' brilliance. It was then that I perceived a phenomenon that I had never experienced before as a human: the union of several separate consciousnesses, each belonging to the luminous forms before me and coming together somewhere inside my mind.

That experience gave new meaning to the word "communion," as it was unlike any form of communication or sharing I had ever known. It was source-to-source, mind-to-mind, and though I found it somewhat overwhelming to process the light beings' impassioned collective thoughts, the preternatural sharing that took place between us was enchanting. It felt like a thousand fireworks exploding at once while my mind attempted to identify each spectacular array of shooting lights and name each new burst of color.

The light beings had greeted me as one mind, one collective consciousness, with only a faint whisper of their individuality discernible in their welcome. While their ethereal light swirled around me and their emotional vitality filled my mind, I was overcome by their unconditional love and the pure joy they expressed in seeing me again. They were my Others, my spiritual family. I knew beyond a doubt that I belonged with them and that I existed as part of their energy, sharing a part of their mind through a cosmic bond.

The rush of panic that I felt during my hypnosis session, when Mr. Dallek told me to say good-bye to the light beings, revealed the depth of that bond: It extended across time, across dimensions. Even after my mind reconnected to physical reality and I sank back into my body, I continued to be pulled toward the light beings' celestial force, and not even Mr. Dallek's suggestion that I relax into a deeper hypnotic state had much effect on the tears that poured from my eyes as I watched my Others fade away. My only comfort in that moment was knowing that I would eventually return to the light beings. I knew that when my physical body ceased to exist, my consciousness—the essence of my being— would be free to rejoin my spiritual family and to live once again in "the light."

Remembering that I was a light being and awakening to my spiritual past was evidently pivotal to events that remained ahead in my human future. During my first hypnosis session, an alien consciousness speaking through me had said, "It is important that she know who she is so she can move on to the next phase of the experiment." When I first spoke those words, I had no idea what they were referring to. But after my second hypnosis session, their meaning was finally made clear, at least the part about knowing my true identity. Not only was I a light being, but an alien consciousness was sharing my existence. That revelation, though shocking, was also something I needed to know.

What remained a mystery, though, was what the alien consciousness had meant by "the next phase of the experiment." Even when I pressed the collective alien consciousness about what they had meant by "wanting me back to complete the studies," they would only say, "You'll understand later," and "It's not your time to know."

Still, the hypnosis sessions brought many of the issues surrounding my involvement with aliens into focus. The sessions also led to insights that I would never have arrived at on my own. For instance, my experiences during hypnosis convinced me that aliens and light beings know each other well and that they exist in a complex and ordered world, though their world was definitely defined by its own unique reality.

Mr. Dallek's particular style of hypnotherapy also proved to be illuminating and therapeutic. He opened my eyes to the true nature of my soul and reminded me that I had free will over my soul. His words led me to realize that it was my thinking—thinking of myself as a helpless victim—that was the genesis of my fears. He also helped me come to terms with those fears and "take back" my nights, so I could return to a normal sleeping pattern.

All that I learned during my hypnosis sessions also changed my thinking about my long history with aliens. If I had agreed to participate in an alien experiment before I was born, the gray beings had probably followed my life from its start, thus explaining why my encounters began in childhood. In retrospect, it seemed that the aliens had gone to a lot of trouble over the years to set into motion whatever it was they still expected me to do. I only wished that I knew the nature of my role in "the next phase of the experiment." If I knew my intended destiny, then at least I could avoid standing in my own way.

The aliens, however, were adamant when they said that it was not my time to know the whole story. There were two things that impressed me about the skinny, gray aliens: first, how quickly they got to their point; secondly, the tone of strict authority that always accompanied their thoughts. It was useless to argue with aliens, at least not the grays. When they said that it was not my time to know, I knew they meant that it was the end of that discussion.

Communicating with the light beings, on the other hand, was by far a more pleasant experience. The information they shared with me seemed more conceptual and open-ended, as if it were up to me to fill in the gaps and to draw my own conclusions, to make sense of it on my own. When asked for information, the light beings just seemed to drop a seed of wisdom into my mind, and it gradually blossomed into concepts that had meaning.

Yet, there were also moments when I found it difficult to grasp what either the aliens or the light beings were trying to tell me. Thoughts and concepts were sometimes conveyed to me at a speed or in a form beyond my perceptual abilities. There were moments when I felt bombarded with data. It was like looking through a kaleidoscope with its ever-changing patterns rotating faster and faster until the images were only a blur. And whenever the light beings spoke into my mind, my desire to simply linger in their energy was so overwhelming that I often lost myself to that feeling. It was difficult to step away from their light, their collective thought energy, and to "think" as an independent consciousness.

In spite of the obstacles, much information did find its way into my awareness from across some dimensional communication channel. I trusted that information, too, because almost all of it was previously unknown—that is, unknown to my human consciousness. I felt certain that the thoughts and emotions flowing into my mind and sometimes into words that magically slipped from my mouth came from a pure source. The light beings' thoughts seemed particularly genuine. Their spiritual radiance was in itself a form of truth, and I regarded the light beings as kindred spirits in the truest sense. The aliens' communications, though harsh and to the point, were also based in their truth. The gray aliens appeared to be completely utilitarian, anyway. Therefore, they didn't mince their thoughts. It was easy to see why the grays had a reputation for being cold and scientific.

Telepathy, the mental transference of consciousness, also instilled a degree of trust to the light beings' and the aliens' communications. This mode of communication—a phenomenon in itself—delivered information directly into my mind. Telepathy actually seemed to increase the reliability of a message, because it provided both conceptual data and the emotional energy that the individual or group mind had attached to the transmission.

The transformational power of standing in the light beings' brilliance, along with the experience of sharing information with the aliens, gradually evolved my spiritual beliefs and pushed my awareness outward toward the dimensional latitudes inherent in my soul. Over time, new concepts started to grow in my mind, and they eventually seeded new questions centering on the meaning of spirituality and the nature of my soul. I wondered, for example, if all humans were light beings. I hoped that was true, then everyone would one day know the extraordinary experience of stepping back into their true form.

But remembering the love the light beings radiated and the passive nature of their energy forced me to wonder how any being that possessed that glorious inner light could cause harm to any other life form, or lie, or deceive, or not care about themselves or the world in which they lived. If all humans possessed that energy, why wasn't the earth a more peaceful, more loving, more promising place?

A few weeks after my second hypnosis session, my question was mysteriously answered.

I watched a newscast highlighting the poverty, strife, and civil unrest raging throughout the world. Stark images of starving, dying children came onto the television screen, and I asked myself yet another question: Why would a light being choose to embark on a human journey if that life was only going to end in a matter of days or weeks or a few years? In the next second, I heard a voice explicitly say, "Not all humans have souls." It was as if a person were standing next to me, but speaking into my mind. *Not all humans have souls?* I was shocked by the notion. I had never considered that possibility before. My Catholic upbringing had insisted otherwise.

I contemplated that idea for a long time. Eventually, I came to understand that not all human organisms are born with a soul. The human organism does, however, arrive with a spiritual intelligence that includes our conscience and our emotions. That form of intelligence, or spiritual essence, links us all to a spiritual source. But that source does not guarantee a soul, nor does it guarantee that when we die, we will step into "the light." Human beings earn that privilege over time, over a period of several lives, or however long it takes.

How we apply our spiritual intelligence and how we express our conscience and nurture and grow our emotional base is the key to spiritual development. Demonstrating love, kindness and goodness; caring for one another and the planet; and acknowledging the spirit in all things are all necessary for soul attainment. But more important than the act—more important than the simple demonstration of kindness, for instance—is *what we think and how we feel.* Anyone can be kind to another person, but what lies unspoken in the individual's consciousness is what counts.

Hence, altruism is one ideal, one paragon for spiritual development. It provides an example of what sets the soul apart from the basic spiritual intelligence. It can be found within beings who practice spiritual responsibility. Spiritual responsibility is aligning your life so you are able to project unselfish love in all directions. Until a human learns how to love in that way, that individual will never attain "soul" status. He or she will have a spiritual essence but will not stand in "the light," not until it achieves a positive, naturally loving, open consciousness.

As for the thousands of starving, dying children whose faces I saw on the television screen, such children are born into circumstances that prevent them from maturing spiritually. There are risks in coming into physical form. I think all spiritual beings know that. The human experience may simply be a process of trial and error, where the spiritual essence is reborn again and again until the conditions are right for spiritual growth.

The more I thought about the dimensional world where light beings and gray aliens exist, the more I could see just how caught up we humans are in our physical reality. Our physical bodies, for example, do not represent who we really are. They are only props that allow us to perform a role while we live out our spiritual journeys. An individual's consciousness, or spiritual essence, simply utilizes the human organism for its purposes. Yet, we humans tend to give more attention to our physical bodies and to our material realities than to our spiritual growth. We don't choose to come into physical form to be perfect biological organisms. We are born into this reality to learn about ourselves as spiritual beings and to develop into souls that eventually become pure light. Perhaps it is at that point in our development when we suddenly have access to the entire universe.

I discovered that my spiritual essence was centered in my thoughts and in my emotions when I stood with the light beings. While communing with my Others, I merged into one collective consciousness. Still, my individual thoughts and feelings represented who I was in that other world. Without a physical body to produce a spoken word, my thoughts and emotions were all that I had to communicate with and all that I had to define "me." Thought and emotion are a form of energy, and that energy is actually very powerful. Even while in human form, my thoughts and emotions, conscious and unconscious, can be heard by beings from across dimensional time and space. It is false to think that consciousness is a private place, nor would we want it to be. If no one could reach us via our consciousness, we would truly exist in isolation. It is all we have when we leave our physical bodies.

The energy in thought and emotion also generates a special kind of language. That unique language is used by aliens and light beings to communicate. I could easily understand why aliens and light beings would refuse to commune with negativity, with hate, with deceit, with selfishness, and with fear. The way they communicate—through telepathy—requires that they consciously "wear" the thoughts and emotions of the individual they are communicating with.

Reaching that understanding helped to explain why the aliens wanted me to learn my true identity. In order for them to communicate with me as a human, a more comfortable pathway or channel had to be created between us. For me, that meant moving beyond my fear and anxiety and returning to the open mind and curious attitude that I once possessed as a child. Thus, if humans wish to communicate with light beings, or with alien life forms, we must all learn to manage our conscious minds. We must remove the barriers from our thoughts and our emotions that impede telepathic communication.

When I first saw the aliens in my parents' bedroom as a little girl, I had not yet learned to fear them. During hypnosis, I had even seen myself as a child walking hand in hand with an alien being. But my human reality had slowly convinced me that such creatures could not be real, and fear grew out of ignorance and false beliefs.

As an adult human, I had to be reminded of my spiritual roots and the agreement I had made with the aliens. Only then could I return to my original understanding of the aliens' purpose in my life and remember that I had nothing to fear. I had to be shown the truth about myself in order to move on to "the next phase of the experiment," and part of my education was to learn that my own thoughts and feelings were standing in the way of my destiny.

That destiny seemed rooted in the light beings' message that I was "like a satellite, radiating light as the sun...keeping energy in balance." Those words seemed to symbolize my role in the aliens' experiment as well as my relationship with the alien consciousness sharing my human life. Somehow, as a light being, I was able to bring the alien energy into this dimension. Perhaps the energy of a light being was necessary to maintain some type of balance between an alien's energy and this world's dimensional plane. Perhaps our individual consciousnesses were placed into one physical body so we could experience two dimensional planes of existence.

The light beings had also said, "You chose to step into their light to discover, to discover yourself." I had stepped into the aliens' light, or life force, to discover my spiritual origins. Clearly, that had been the result. Without the bizarre alien encounters in my life, it's unlikely that I would have ended up in a hypnotherapist's office, searching for solutions to overcome my fears and end my sleepless nights. The aliens' intentions to bring me into another dimension of time and space during my first hypnosis session was also apparent, and it was there that I discovered my true self.

When Mr. Dallek had asked whether or not the essence of my being was one and the same as the energy and the essence of the alien being, the alien consciousness had said, "No, it's similar. She's been altered." I wasn't sure what "altered" meant or how that had been accomplished, but I strongly sensed that my encounters with aliens were responsible for my alterations. Perhaps the aliens were gradually altering my physical body to accommodate the alien consciousness so her energy could more fully experience being in human form.

Everything I had learned about aliens through direct experience or from books about alien contact supported the notion that these nonhuman beings had their own unique physics. As humans, we have defined the properties of matter, energy, motion, and force only as they relate to our physical world, not how they exist in other dimensions. It would seem that in an alien's world, where beings move through solid matter as if it were air, aliens could effect any number of alterations on a human body, both physical and psychical. Or maybe I had been genetically altered to accommodate physical human form and the aliens were monitoring the results while continuing their experiment. Some alien abduction researchers believed that at least some aliens were conducting genetic studies on humans.

Yet, when Mr. Dallek asked if the aliens' experiment was the implant of an alien essence into physical form to see what would develop, the alien consciousness had replied, "Partly," as if there were more to the story. I sensed that my alien counterpart was holding something back. But since it was not in an alien's nature to be deliberately mysterious, I was sure she had her reasons if she were appropriating information. And sharing mental space with the alien consciousness didn't make me privy to what was in her mind. She also had free will to direct her thoughts and emotions as she chose, though there were moments when her individual thoughts would suddenly merge with my psyche and her emotions would overlap my own.

It was this overlapping of emotions, and sometimes the extreme switching of emotions, that enabled me to know without a doubt that the alien's thoughts were separate from my own. I had experienced that sensation during past alien encounters, most dramatically, during the two encounters when I saw the spaceships hovering in the sky. Of course, during those events, I never understood why it seemed as though another person was suddenly standing inside my physical body. And there were other times when I wondered why I would think that it was perfectly normal to wake up and find strange beings next to my bed. Yet, it was because I could remember what it felt like to have a completely different consciousness think and emote alongside my human awareness that I could believe that an alien consciousness was sharing my human existence.

Nevertheless, accepting the presence of a separate consciousness within the regions of my own mind rocked what few paradigms were left standing in my world. Sometimes I would study my face in a mirror and wonder what kind of abomination I was looking at. But in the reflection I saw the same face that had always stared back at me. It was the face of a human female whose features I had scrutinized a million times. Yet something was different about me, something had changed. Something inside of me, inside the core of my being, had been awakened, and the only way I could see what a mirror could not show me was to close my human eyes. There in the dim light of some other world was a different reflection. And while staring into dark, round eyes and surveying the gray, oval head, I knew that some part of me was pleased to again look upon *her* face.

Living with another mind, a distinctly different conscious energy, had little impact on my day-to-day life. My human consciousness was almost always in the forefront of my awareness. After all, as a human being, I was living in *my* world and in *my* dimension. Coping with the alien's presence required few changes in how I interacted with my physical environment. That was not the case, however, for my alien self. I soon realized that she was struggling with her awareness of my physical world.

I discovered her feelings around that issue not long after my second hypnosis session. The layer of consciousness belonging to my alien counterpart rose to the surface of my human mind and spoke to me. "Like limbo," she said. "Trapped in duty to serve the species. Home. Want to go home to the others, to be in connection with their energies, to touch souls again with the species."

I grabbed a notebook and a pen from my coffee table and quickly jotted down her unexpected, yet unmistakable words. To me, they sounded like a wistful lamentation. It immediately melted the core of my human identity, allowing a thin icing of sorrow to drizzle down over my soul. For a moment, a potent yearning to be elsewhere blanketed my mind, and before I could finish recording the message that had streamed across my consciousness, a pang of isolation pierced my human heart.

Trapped. My alien consciousness had selected that particular word from my vocabulary to describe its earthbound plight. She felt trapped inside a human form to carry out a duty. Though willingly chosen, that obligation forced a prolonged and painful separation from the world she once knew.

I had been sitting on the couch in my living room, silently meditating on the nature of souls, when the alien voice shot through my mind. The sudden projection of that distinctive voice alongside my human thoughts startled me. Yet, as it reached into my mental space, tapping into and projecting out through my emotions, it was overwhelmingly clear that the alien consciousness was intertwined within the whole of my being.

My human awareness, however, contained no grief or disappointment in response to the circumstance of being human. But the alien aspect of my psyche was definitely sad, nearly despondent. The juxtaposition of our two mindsets during that moment reinforced my belief that a separate consciousness shared residence within my physical form.

As a human being, I could not completely comprehend how that had been made possible. I decided that it could only be explained within the context of another dimension's laws and principles—a world where energy equals a powerful spiritual force rather than Einstein's mc^2. From my hypnosis experiences, I knew that in the dimension where my alien consciousness came from and where light beings roamed, the properties defining the mechanics and dynamics of mass were not bound by earth's rigid physics. For an alien, awakening to the limitations of a human's physical reality was probably similar to how a human would feel if forced to live in a cage.

There were extreme differences between my human world and the alien's dimensional reality. Thinking about those differences reminded me of something the light beings had said during my second hypnosis session. When I asked them for information about my role in the agreement I had made with the aliens, they said that my understanding would "allow me to cope with the realities of my being who I am." It suddenly occurred to me that my job was to help the alien consciousness cope with her shifting reality. It was my role to balance her energy, balance her mind, while she slowly adjusted to the human experience.

At that point in time, the only way I could compare how the alien perceived reality with how I perceived mine was to recall my experience when the squadron of spaceships appeared. A wealth of knowledge had poured into my mind. It seemed as if I had been given a key that could unlock the great mysteries of the universe. There was also an incredible sense of joy in connecting with the people inside the ships. Collectively, those perceptions were woven together into an extraordinary conceptual tapestry. If the alien consciousness experienced that marvelous tapestry as its natural waking state, my human mind was a blank canvas in comparison. Even the young girl that I was at that time wanted to return to the alien's state of awareness after the event. When the ships were in the sky, I was happier than I had ever been.

It occurred to me that the alien consciousness sharing my existence had probably sacrificed the powerful connections it once shared with its alien family in order to experience a human life. As a light being, I had made that sacrifice too, and during my first hypnosis session, I also expressed overwhelming grief in the moments prior to being dimensionally separated from the light energies I knew as my Others. I could relate to the alien's wish to go home. But as I sat on my couch that afternoon, listening to the alien mind express its reaction to being in my human reality, I could not relate to the heaviness attached to her concept of duty or to the extreme sense of isolation she projected into my mind.

The alien consciousness definitely missed her home. She communicated that message to me through human words dipped in sorrow. The poignant longing that coated the alien's thoughts stirred up in me the memory of a peculiar alien form I had seen in a dream. That being had been struggling along a dirt path, inching its way toward a huge nest that contained several large eggs. When the strange creature gently spread itself over the eggs in a manner that spoke of endings, of death, sorrow and longing had filled my heart at that time, too. I wondered if the creature represented my alien self. Had the deep, lasting sorrow that weighed down on my heart arisen from the alien's grief over its own death? Did the eggs represent her lost offspring in some way or the extinction of a life form?

Still positioned on my couch, pen and paper still in hand, I listened to the now familiar voice respond to my meandering thoughts. "The sadness you experienced was not a reflection on the mortality of the species," the alien consciousness said. "It was a response of longing to be in the embrace of my own kind. How abandoned I feel in this body. Left."

The sudden emergence of the alien consciousness into my stream of thought gave me the idea that perhaps she would answer other questions I still had about my bizarre alien encounters and dream-like experiences. I questioned the alien consciousness about the significance of the squadron of spaceships seen during childhood.

"Ships. So glad to see them," was her response. "They filled the sky above me like angels hovering over, watching. Brief contact. Then away they go, leaving me behind."

"But why did they come? Why do the aliens still come for us?" I asked in earnest, hoping to gain a clearer understanding of what must lie ahead in the future.

"I know why, but I can't tell you. It is still not your time to know."

My next question naturally followed the alien's shielded response. "When?" I asked. "When will it be my time?"

"Soon," the alien consciousness told me. Then, she added, "Be patient. It will be a wonderful surprise."

That conversation launched a strange, but special relationship between two minds from different worlds. Over time, the alien and I began to learn how to stand in each other's "light." I discovered things about her nature, while she explored the human condition and the emotional playground native to a human soul.

There were, of course, a few fundamental concepts I already understood about aliens. My previous experiences with these unique creatures had provided some insight into their unusual ways. I learned things about the gray aliens by observing their behaviors; or while mentally positioned next to my alien counterpart's mind; or while connected with the aliens' collective consciousness, or group mind, as I had done during my hypnosis sessions. I actually found the beings to be quite fascinating.

From my point of view, the aliens' most distinctive behavioral characteristic was their lack of emotional expression. Emotion was absent from their faces, and it was never visible in their body language. I could still see in my mind the skinny, gray creatures standing in attention, assuming that rigid, military-like bearing, just seconds before the light beings' brilliant forms appeared. Minutes later, when I observed the row of aliens again, they were still displaying the same stiff posture, their dark, round eyes fixed on the light beings positioned straight ahead. That vacant, wide-eyed stare reminded me of the peculiar expression I had seen on the faces of the creatures who marched into my parents' bedroom when I was a three-year-old child. It was an expression void of emotion, a face without a story, and it always left me with the impression that aliens emitted very little energy and their temperaments were extremely flat. When the light beings appeared, my face beamed with joy and excitement at the sight of the shimmering forms.

I often wondered if the gray aliens' lack of emotional expression and lethargic behavior were due to a lack of emotion or simply due to a lack of passion. Humans as well as light beings—as I discovered—are extremely passionate beings, and our passion enables us to project emotion far out beyond our inner light. When the light beings floated toward me during my first hypnosis session, their impassioned greeting felt like a shockwave. The light beings' emotional effervescence easily made up for the aliens' lack of personality.

The gray aliens and the light beings were obviously very different life forms. Yet during the time I stood in the aliens' dimensional realm, I sensed a definite relationship between the two types of beings. It was obvious that they could coexist in the same dimension, and they recognized each other in spite of the extreme variance in their energy forms. The light beings even emitted what I perceived to be an open, trusting attitude toward the gray aliens. And from the vantage point of the collective alien consciousness, I sensed that the aliens regarded the light beings as spiritual cousins, too.

The aliens' attitude toward humans, though, was a different matter. Their collective consciousness explicitly held the attitude that humans were subordinates, and the aliens' telepathic thought energy expressed that quite firmly. Yet, in spite of their attitude, there was nothing aggressive about the aliens' thoughts, nothing that could be construed as a threat to the human species. I strongly doubted that aliens had the equivalent of the human ego, anyway. They seemed to be motivated by a group mind, rather than the individual self. Hence, I thought it was unlikely that warmongers and power-hungry zealots would be found within their ranks.

My impression was that the gray aliens were exceptionally pragmatic. Everything in their world had a purpose, a practical purpose, a collective purpose. I could sense it in their task-centered, robot-like behavior. It was even recognizable in the way the aliens communicated. Without a stew of emotions complicating their minds, their thoughts came through as sharply focused ideas and concepts carved out of their pragmatic logic.

For instance, when Mr. Dallek asked me during my second hypnosis session if the aliens' light was one and the same as the light of humans, I responded by saying, "No, their light is different." Since that answer had been provided to me by the alien consciousness rather than derived from my human intellect, my mind naturally searched for an explanation. I telepathically posed another question, inquiring what made their light different. The collective alien consciousness offered me a broad response, one that centered on the word "purpose." I heard them say that their purpose was "well defined," whereas humans had "no purpose." That was their way of answering my question, though it left a huge gap in my understanding.

When my human consciousness searched into their mental space for further explanation, I found only an attitude that seemed to say: *We provided you with the answer; it's not our fault if you don't understand it.* The alien arrogance, the haughtiness, that often carried the beings' thoughts, presented itself again.

Even the aliens' superior attitude toward humans seemed more like a statement of fact than an opinion open for debate, though. It was not meant to incite an argument. There was nothing malicious backing the aliens' conscious energy, only solid, fundamental alien beliefs.

Of course, there was always the possibility that the labels I gave the aliens' telepathic communications—arrogant, haughty, superior—were reflections of my own emotional reactions to the thoughts projected into my mind. After all, I was translating the aliens' flat, matter-of-fact thought energy through my human consciousness. As a human, I perceived thought energy from an emotional perspective, whereas aliens appeared to be almost emotionless. With that major difference dividing our conversations, I may have been judging the aliens' thoughts. I wasn't sure if I knew how to separate emotion from my thoughts. It seemed to me that emotion is to human consciousness as oxygen is to air, and human survival depends upon both to about the same degree.

From an aliens' perspective, their comments about humans were probably offered as unadorned facts, especially if it was true that within their culture all individual behavior is driven by the collective group mind. Under those conditions, every thought and every action would describe the aliens' unified purpose, and they would interact with other species from a "what you see is what we are" behavioral platform.

Humans, of course, operate from a completely different psychology. Our individualism and independent thinking set us apart from the gray aliens. They would probably regard those traits as unnecessary, possibly viewing them as primitive aspects of our biology. Without an understanding of our need for self-expression and creativity, aliens would probably view human behavior as chaotic, unpredictable, and perhaps even dangerous. They might think that humans have no purpose because they see that we have a million purposes. The multiplicity of human nature would be as "alien" to aliens as their group behavior and their single-purpose mentality would be to us.

That difference alone could have explained the aliens' barbed attitude toward humans. Just as I may have been making emotional judgments about the aliens' attitude, they in turn could have been making judgments toward humans based on their dispassionate and pragmatic view of our behavior and our world.

Attempting to understand the alien psyche and to identify the intrinsic differences between aliens and humans helped me gauge how the alien consciousness sharing my human realm might be reacting to the forces around her. Coming from a world that communicated telepathically, she would be accustomed to the immediate access, if not the continuous presence, of several minds at any given time. She would know the intimacy of mingling inside another person's mind or even a collective consciousness in its entirety. To wake up inside a physical body—with only spoken words with which to communicate—the outer physical world would certainly be a shock to an alien, and realizing that you are the only energy inside your awareness would make your conscious reality a very lonely place.

In contrast, human beings are not accustomed to sharing mental space with anyone. And hearing a voice that isn't coming from either a physical, mechanical, or electronic source would be frightening to some people, while others would simply dismiss it and think that they must have imagined the sound.

In past centuries, when people claimed to hear voices, it was believed that the voices belonged to demons or evil spirits. There was even a time when these people were burned at the stake. Today, hearing voices is often associated with psychopathology and psychotic disorders such as schizophrenia. (Psychotic disorders, of course, do include delusions and hallucinations.) It's obvious why humans in modern Western society would be fearful of telepathic communications. It's also obvious why the concept of dual consciousness might be feared.

For me, embracing such concepts had necessitated no less than a quantum leap of faith. They did not easily fit into the culture that had defined my human reality. For most of my life, I had gone along with the scientific paradigm that demanded hard evidence as proof of everything. For much of that time, I also believed that humans might actually be the only intelligent life in the universe. Because I'd been entrenched in that singular, myopic view for so many years, I was a perfect specimen in which aliens could observe human attitudinal change.

I spent nearly a year evolving through denial and wrestling with my human fears before I was ready to accept the existence of aliens and my involvement in the alien abduction phenomenon. The aliens who were watching me would have learned that new beliefs and changing realities did not easily penetrate a human's cultural and scientific foundations. The only reason I adopted a new view of reality was because it was constantly shoved in front of my face.

The aliens would have also witnessed my process of acceptance and growth. Once I let go of my outdated beliefs and actually took a good look at the dimensional universe around me, I was ready to move on to another level within my cosmic school. I had finally reached an important milestone: emotional, intellectual, and spiritual readiness. Without those factors in place, my psyche would not have possessed the maturity necessary to maintain an open mind, and I would not have been ready to participate in what was yet to come.

My old attitudes and belief system had to change if I was ever to accept the fact that an alien consciousness was sharing my life. That concept was just too absurd, when measured against traditional Western beliefs, to be readily accepted. Yet, for alien life forms—whose scientific paradigms allowed them to dart around in spaceships, walk through walls, and float people out of their homes in beams of light—it was perfectly normal, even simple.

With such broad differences between alien and human worlds, I had to assume that the alien consciousness would have an opinion about me—the human "me"—and about life in a physical body. If it were true that our individual consciousnesses had been together since birth, then she would have gained much knowledge about the human condition while waiting for me, a human baby, to mature through childhood and adolescence, and eventually become an adult.

Thinking about the alien consciousness sharing my early life jarred the memory of my mother telling me that I skipped over my childhood. "You went from diapers to playing school," she had said. "You never played with dolls."

I could recall the countless hours spent in the basement of the farmhouse, sitting at a small wooden desk, surrounded by the tools of a young student—paper, pens, pencils, erasers, crayons, and chalk. With my head bent over the basic readers that had come from the country school down the road, I ardently memorized the words describing the antics of three children named Dick, Jane, and Sally, who were seldom without their little dog, Spot. When I wasn't practicing the fundamentals of reading, writing, and arithmetic, I was impatiently waiting to grow up, waiting to complete the slow and tedious developmental process required of all humans so I could get on with my life.

My formative years, now memories wrapped in the sweet innocence of youth and layered with happiness and reminiscences of fun-filled times, were often spent yearning for the freedom that adults appeared to possess. I constantly struggled to assert my independence and autonomy, while loathing the constraints that my young age placed on me. As far back as I could remember, my desire to dictate my own life steered much of my behavior, and I never understood why I had to have permission to do what I wanted to do, to have what I wanted to have, or to be who I wanted to be. Fortunately for my family, by the age of five, I had learned to behave myself, but only after discovering that the world was a more harmonious place when I behaved like a child rather than a tyrant.

"Someday you'll regret that you were never a child," my mother would say. But if the alien consciousness had been listening, she probably would have retorted, "I don't care. I just want to get this phase over with." Today, the question remains: Exactly who had more influence over my childhood behavior—my human psyche or the alien consciousness?

It was this independent spirit, though, that probably provided common ground on which my alien consciousness and my human awareness were first able to relate. Acknowledging our likenesses also tightened the gap between our uniquely different worlds, making it easier to step in and out of each others' dimensional experience.

The alien consciousness and I seemed to be taking turns teaching each other new things about our divergent worlds. Her education took place in my human reality, and my lessons took place in another dimension of space and time. Apparently, I still had much to learn, because within weeks of my second hypnosis session, I had another encounter with aliens. And during the year that followed, mysterious wonders continued to appear, leading me along a path of greater enlightenment.

CHAPTER 8

Emerging into the Night

ACROSS A SPAN OF THREE DECADES the little gray aliens had been showing up in my world, always at night, always unannounced, and always going about their business with a swiftness, a silence, and a kind of magic that mimicked the nocturnal emergence of bats. I rarely ever held the aliens in my gaze, yet, whenever they happened to wake me from sleep, I never doubted that they were near. I felt their presence. I felt their bodies moving around me in the same way you can sense an impending electrical storm.

The aliens' arrival during the early hours of July 26, 1992, was much the same, and again they prevented me from getting a glimpse of their forms as they hovered over my body. Yet there was something different about this particular encounter, something that set it apart from other visitations. That difference was a small blunder the aliens made that proved to me that these peculiar nonhuman creatures could not only enter the three-dimensional world of humans, but they could alter our environment as well, leaving behind physical evidence of their presence.

Never before had my involvement in the alien abduction phenomenon convinced me that my interactions with aliens occurred on a physical plane and in my material world. In spite of once watching an alien entourage file into a room, in spite of observing unidentified beings standing next to my bed, and in spite of locking eyes with a gray alien whose face once appeared from around a corner, I was never absolutely sure if the strange creatures had solid, corporeal bodies or if they were merely ethereal entities manifesting in a humanoid form. But after one unsettling summer night, I never questioned that issue again.

The encounter took place in Wisconsin, on a farm belonging to Jean and Joe Edlin, my sister and brother-in-law. Their dairy operation sat atop the bluffs overlooking the Mississippi River. The river wasn't visible from the Edlins' main farmstead, but on a clear day, while standing in their front yard, you could see for miles across the valley below. It was a spectacular twenty-mile vista.

In another direction, you could see the Edlins' driveway, a mile-long stretch of gravel. During the summer, parallel strips of corn and alfalfa rolled across the adjacent fields to where they eventually butted up against lush green woodland borders. The end of the drive led past the horse pasture and continued on up the hill to where two majestic silos towered over the red cow barn. Advancing several more feet brought you to the terraced yard, where a flower garden annually displayed its colorful bounty. Climbing the steps to the next level took you along a short pathway that led to the house.

Except for the milk hauler, the farm employees, and occasional visitors such as insurance agents, seed salesmen, and friends, few people had reason to leave the main highway and travel the three miles to the Edlins' isolated farm. As one of those occasional visitors and a frequent weekend guest, I appreciated the isolated aspect of the farm's location. Besides being a picturesque rural paradise, the Edlins' farm offered a welcomed escape from my city existence. I had been retreating to its rustic beauty for many years.

It never occurred to me, though, that the unpredictable aliens would appreciate the farm's isolation, too. But it was a perfect setting for an alien abduction, and over time I would come to believe that my short, gray interlopers actually preferred it over other places I often escaped to. On the night of the encounter, the Edlins' farm presented an even more ideal location for an abduction. Only three people were in the house—my sister, her seven-year-old son, and me.

Earlier that week, Jean had telephoned to ask if I wanted to drive down from Minneapolis and spend a day or two at the farm. "Everyone's going fishing," she said, "so I'll be all alone. I'd like the company."

My brother-in-law was taking his two young sons on a weekend fishing trip. But Todd, who wasn't as keen on fishing as his older brother Tony, decided at the last minute to stay home.

When I arrived at the farm it was already mid-afternoon on Saturday. Todd was playing outside in the yard, and after I brought my luggage into the house, he joined me on a tour of the vegetable and flower gardens. Jean was busy with farm chores, so Todd and I amused ourselves by wandering around the grounds, looking for something of interest. We eventually found our way to the basketball hoop where we shot baskets for a while.

By the time Jean had finished feeding and milking the cows, the sun was already lapping at the horizon. Since we had not eaten supper yet, we decided to build a fire in the outdoor fireplace and transform the evening into a picnic.

It was a grand summer night, and we took full advantage of the warm air and clear evening skies by spending the entire evening outdoors. The mosquitoes were merciful that evening; even in July their constant buzzing and biting can ruin the most pleasant picnic. Those that did find us were kept back by the heat of our popping fire, so we positioned our three lawn chairs close to the flames.

Jean, Todd, and I snacked on fresh garden vegetables while heating hot dogs and, later, marshmallows over the burning logs. Todd was bent on catching fireflies, so Jean and I occasionally interrupted our conversation to report a firefly sighting, yelling, "There. No, wait. There it is. No, now it's over there," while pointing toward the dots of light flashing on and off among the stalks of field corn that grew just beyond the edge of the lawn. Todd, butterfly net in hand, would then dash off in the reported direction.

But as darkness gradually replaced the evening light, the visibility around the three of us shrunk down to where we could no longer see where the lawn ended and the farm fields began. Only Domino, the family's German shepherd, and Betsy, a dog belonging to my brother-in-law's fishing partner, cared to venture into the murky space.

Though I continued to gab with my sister, I found myself mentally tracking the dogs' whereabouts. Having them nearby abated the slight tingling that crawled along the base of my spine whenever I glanced out into the surrounding blackness. I wondered if anything was out there watching our intimate threesome, two women and a small boy. Yet I knew the dogs would certainly alert us with barks and growls, or maybe even a cowardly retreat, if that were true.

But all remained calm while we chatted and enjoyed the blazing fire.

Eventually, we gathered up our picnic leftovers and tossed our used paper plates into the fireplace. Flames shot up into the air one more time, helping to light our way across the yard as we headed toward the house.

It was close to 10:30 p.m. An hour later, the three of us were cleaned up, tucked in our beds, and dozing off to sleep.

Sleep came. Then suddenly the night split open with sound. It was my sister's voice against a background of savage barking.

"Domino, shut up! Get in your doghouse," Jean yelled. I could tell by her tone that she was annoyed.

But the noise continued. Both Domino and Betsy were barking and growling angrily, cutting apart what had been a peaceful sleep. One dog was outside the house, the other, much closer. I learned from Jean in the morning that Betsy, the aging cocker spaniel, was standing on her bed, her front paws resting on the window ledge while barking in chorus with Domino, who was pacing on the lawn below.

I could see from my nephew's lighted alarm clock that it was 1:23 a.m. I'd been asleep only a couple of hours when Domino's thundering discharge and Betsy's echoing yelps blasted me into consciousness.

Todd was lying on the lower trundle bed that was partly tucked under my bed frame at a ninety-degree angle. He squirmed for a few seconds, as if searching for a different sleeping position, before settling back into a motionless form.

Jean gave the dogs another stern reprimand, commanding Betsy to come away from the window and return to her spot on the bed. Domino had to be scolded again before he obediently stopped his barking. Even then, he continued to growl, producing deep, throaty sounds that still carried an edge of wariness.

Minutes later, both dogs were silent, and my heart returned to a quieter rhythm. It wasn't long before I slipped into unconsciousness for the second time that night.

When I opened my eyes again, several bodies were moving around in the darkness.

I was lying on my stomach, fully stretched out across the mattress. Although my body seemed frozen in that position, I was intensely aware of the pair of bony fingers that were tucked under the top edge of the spandex running shorts I had worn to bed.

Two hard digits were pressed against my flesh. I felt them just beneath my waistline, toward the outer edges of my hips. Whoever was touching me must have been short, because I sensed that the arms were reaching out over my lower body while resting on the edge of the upper trundle bed.

In the seconds I recorded what was happening around me, there was absolutely no fear within my mind. Once again that emotion was strangely missing from a scene that should have been marked by terror, especially since I thought that a piece of my clothing was about to be removed. Instead, my awareness simply registered an alien presence in the room, and I calmly accepted my circumstances in the familiar manner I had come to associate with these unexpected bedside visits.

Within seconds, I was no longer awake.

The next thing I saw was the morning, and it was a beautiful day. The sun was shining; the birds were chirping. I could hear cows bellowing nearby and off in the distance, as herds of Holsteins began their morning milking routine.

I lounged in bed for a while, soaking in the sounds and smells of nature coming in through the open window. But I was thinking about the night. Domino and Betsy had created quite a scene. I wondered if their intense barking and the quickening of my pulse had fueled my imagination and prompted an experience that played out as an alien encounter. I hadn't actually seen any beings in the room during the night. I had only sensed bodies and heard noises that I perceived as movement in the room.

Then I remembered that I had felt two bony fingers against my lower back. It had been my impression that someone was trying to remove my shorts.

Recalling that curious sensation triggered an odd question: If the aliens had actually paid me another visit and removed the tight-fitting spandex shorts I had worn to bed, would they have known that the shorts were on backwards?

I was never sure whether it was the cut of the fabric or the shorts' particular design that encouraged this, but the pair of black running shorts I had worn to bed that night fit better if they were on backwards. I always checked to see that the fabric tag was in the front before slipping the shorts over my hips.

Whoever removed my shorts during the night hadn't been aware of that detail. I discovered that my shorts had been turned around. The fabric tag was now at my back, and that was not where it had been when I crawled into bed.

The physical evidence the aliens had left in their wake darkened my sunny mood. Not wanting to believe that I had been touched by alien hands, I searched for another reason to explain this new mystery.

I explored the possibility that maybe I hadn't put my running shorts on backwards. Yet, as I walked back in my mind to the time I dressed for bed, I knew that the fit of the shorts alone would have told me which way I was wearing them on my body, as they were noticeably uncomfortable if worn the regular way. I had also walked around in them that night, and long enough to know their position.

I also knew that the only reason I bothered to check the location of the shorts' fabric tag in the morning was because I detected someone's fingers underneath the waistband during the night. And, everything I remembered about the queer experience, everything I perceived during approximately ten to fifteen seconds of consciousness, coincided with what I had come to recognize over the years as an alien encounter. The one varying feature during this encounter, however, was that someone else was in the room: my seven-year-old nephew Todd.

From across the breakfast table that morning, I examined my nephew's face, looking for a sign or an expression that might tell me if something was on his mind. Todd was a handsome boy despite the yet uncombed dark hair sticking out in tufts from the top of his head. He flashed his blue eyes in my direction, but they revealed nothing more than their normal mischievous twinkle.

Todd and I finished our bowls of cereal. Then we strolled out into the fresh country air to pick raspberries, each equipped with an empty plastic container. After navigating the flower garden, with a stop along the way to search for the goldfish in the garden pond, we found our way to the red raspberry patch.

I could not get the evening's strange events out of my mind, so I decided to ask Todd if he had witnessed anything unusual during the night.

"How did you sleep?" I asked my nephew, attempting to ease into a casual conversation. "Did you hear Domino and Betsy barking?"

Todd popped a ripe raspberry into his mouth, then dropped the next one he found into his white plastic berry bowl. "Yeah, they sure made a lot of noise," he said, pressing his lips down over another plump red berry. "Betsy was sleeping in Jeannie's bedroom." (My nephews occasionally referred to their parents by their first names.)

"I know," I said, noticing that my pickings were quickly outnumbering Todd's by two to one. Limiting my search to only the choicest berries, I tossed the next few that I pulled from the bushes into my mouth. Then I got to the question I most wanted to ask, "Todd, did you have any dreams last night?"

The row of berry bushes that separated Todd and me partially shielded his face. I stepped into the thicket of prickly branches, positioning myself across from where he stood in order to gauge any reaction that might arise from my question.

My nephew immediately responded, though his expression remained unchanged. "I had two dreams last night," he told me, while continuing to search for red berries among the green leaves. "I had one good dream and one bad dream."

"What was the bad dream about?" I asked, then realized that I should have inquired about the good dream first. The look on my nephew's young face suddenly changed, and a prolonged silence trailed after my question.

When Todd finally spoke, what he said was completely unexpected. "I don't want to tell you," came my nephew's sheepish voice.

It was not my intention to invade the privacy of a seven-year-old's dream world, so I waited before pressing the issue any further. The silence held for nearly a minute, and during that time Todd stopped picking berries. He just stared into the branches that reached up past his face, and the playful smile that had defined his prior disposition now appeared pinched by whatever was running through his mind.

Without looking up at me, he suddenly added, "I don't want to tell you because...because something bad happened to *you* in the dream."

The cautious manner in which he delivered his words released into my heart a flood of affection. I knew then why my sweet, sensitive little nephew did not want to share his bad dream: He was trying to protect me from its content.

Todd glanced up for a brief moment to meet my eyes, and I released to him a smile that expressed my heart. Then we both went back to picking berries.

I searched through my mind for the right thing to say to soften the subject of our conversation. Todd's dream had, of course, intrigued me, and I wanted to know more about it.

"You know, I sometimes have bad dreams, too," I said. "Everyone has them, so it's okay to tell me about your bad dream, if you want to."

Not a single word was offered during the next thirty seconds, and Todd's reticence caused me to wonder if I really wanted to know what he obviously was not comfortable divulging. I was about to completely drop the subject when Todd finally shared with me what had been on his mind.

"Well, I guess...I guess I can tell you," Todd said, though his reluctance was still audible in his voice. "I dreamed, umm, that a big sea monster came into the bedroom last night. It swallowed you up and took you away."

If I had heard such a line under other circumstances, I probably would have laughed aloud and goaded my nephew for the gruesome details of my demise in the jaws of the sea monster. But the serious tone in which Todd related the dream and his reluctance to share it with me cast a grim shadow of reality over the dream scenario. His story ran parallel to my suspicion that I had been abducted during the night. I made no attempt at comic relief. Instead, I spent the next few seconds searching for a way to continue the conversation without burdening my nephew with the emotional fallout from my own eclipsing mood. I came up with what I hoped would sound like an innocuous question.

"What did the monster look like?" I asked. "Did it have any eyes?"

"It had eleven eyes," Todd said confidently, as if he had actually counted them.

The rising summer sun was slowly evaporating what was left of the morning dew. But the moisture that had been clinging to the grass earlier in the day had slowly seeped into my canvas sneakers. Maybe it was because that dampness had finally reached the soles of my feet, but as I silently speculated on what Todd might have witnessed during the night, a sudden chill came over my body.

"It swallowed you up and took you away," my nephew had said, describing the actions of the sea monster in his dream. For a moment, the sensation of bony fingers pressing down against my flesh came back into my mind, and then it was my turn to withhold my inner thoughts.

I decided not to pump my nephew for any more details about the sea monster. It would have only heightened the tension the bad dream had evoked in him, anyway. And I had learned what I originally set out to discover: whether or not my nephew had experienced anything unusual during the night. The implications of Todd's dream were already creating a dry lump in my throat. I only hoped that my nephew had not been involved in the abduction, too.

Even though I had accepted my involvement in the alien abduction phenomenon, I was not ready to accept the possibility that it could extend into the lives of the people around me. The idea that aliens might touch the people I loved and cared about did not sit comfortably with me. I especially did not want my young nephews to be exposed to the aliens' ways, mostly out of concern that they might experience the same anxiety and fear that had invaded my adult life.

While standing in the raspberry patch, I reminded myself that Todd's "monster" might have been just a dream and not a child's version of an alien abduction scene. But as hard as I tried to bring that possibility into focus, it did not explain the peculiar events that had taken place during the night. Something had startled the dogs; someone's fingers had pressed down on the back of my hips; and someone had plainly removed my running shorts, then put them back on my body the wrong way.

The odd incident that took place in my nephew's bedroom also paralleled events I had read about that described typical abduction scenarios. It was easy to fill in the gaps between my perceptions and Todd's dream from the list of bizarre behaviors that profiled the aliens' typical mode of operation: Aliens often removed abductees' clothing; aliens could "shut down" animals as well as people while an abduction took place; and aliens frequently demonstrated mental capabilities far beyond those yet achieved by humans.

It was more likely that the sea monster Todd had seen taking me from the bedroom was part of an alien-induced dreamscape masking events that the alien beings did not want a young boy to see or remember. Based upon the accounts of alien abduction I had read, abductees seemed to agree that these unusual creatures were quite adept at influencing what went on in a human's mind, and when it came to disguise, aliens were experts.

But attention to detail? Well, considering that the alien beings had made a mistake when they slipped my formfitting running shorts back over my hips, that particular attribute did not appear to be one of their strengths. Or had they purposely left that clue behind as physical proof of their visit?

Was it possible that the alien beings were slowly trying to prove their existence to humans who instinctively sought other explanations to explain their bizarre encounters? Had aliens finally reached the conclusion that to get our attention, to shake us out of our closet realities and open our minds, they would have to resort to *our* extremes?

If proving their existence had been one of the aliens' goals in their continuing interactions with me, they had finally reached it. Actually, I had stopped doubting their existence a long while back. But after the encounter in my nephew's bedroom, I also stopped doubting their *physical* existence. It was now obvious to me that alien life forms could walk through walls, then become solid bodies. Aliens were more than ethereal beings. They had proven to me that they could physically influence my human reality: They could remove my clothes; they could physically touch my flesh.

Still, everything in my physical reality was the same after the encounter. There were no marks on my body. No evidence was found to suggest that intruders had been in the house. Even the dogs were the same frisky pets they had been on the day before. And much to my comfort, my nephew's spunky behavior returned soon after our conversation about the night and his bad dream had ended.

As the day went on, my own mood gradually lifted, and the night's alien mystery faded from my thoughts. I had nearly forgotten about the strange incident by the time I saw my brother-in-law's truck coming up the long driveway, signaling the fishermen's return.

Within minutes, Tony was bounding up the steps toward the house, arms laden with packages filled with gifts for his younger brother.

It was then that I recalled what Todd had told me about the other dream he had remembered from the night. "In my good dream," my nephew had said, "Tony came home from the fishing trip, and he had lots of presents for me."

Maybe it was just a coincidence, and I didn't want to believe that this event could have any bearing on the darker events my nephew had dreamed about during the night, but Todd's good dream had obviously come true.

CHAPTER 9

Lessons in Dimensional Reality

THE TWELVE MONTHS THAT FOLLOWED the aliens' visit to the Edlins' farm were filled with strange, yet enlightening events. There were days when I felt as though I were living in a never-ending episode of Rod Serling's *Twilight Zone,* where high strangeness and unpredictability reigned. I had experienced weird and unexplainable happenings before, of course, but after the encounter that occurred in my nephews' bedroom, the frequency of bizarre incidents seemed to increase. Or, maybe I was just getting better at detecting the moments when my physical reality collided with some other dimension.

In retrospect, my life had never been the perfect picture of normality that I had assumed it was. Even while I was growing up on my parents' dairy farm in Wisconsin, there were occasions when the impossible presented itself. Looking back through those years, I could locate several bizarre incidents. They were filed away in my memory drawer labeled *I Can't Explain It, I Just Know It Happened.*

One of the most bewildering and frightening of those impossible events took place during my early adolescence. The incident happened on a Saturday morning while my older sisters and I were in the midst of our weekly cleaning chores. It was my turn to vacuum—rather than dust—that day, and I needed the vacuum cleaner that was kept in the large walk-in storage room located on the second floor of the farmhouse.

Clearing two steps at a time, I bounded up the stairway. The entrance to the storeroom was at the top of the stairs. With my hand still gripping the door handle, I leaned into the room, turned on the overhead light, and surveyed the layers of stuff.

It was a typical storage room with storm windows, old toys, dust-covered knickknacks, and boxes containing things that had been discarded or were seldom used. At least a half-dozen winter coats hung from the clothes rod that stretched across the back wall. Interspersed between the coats were a variety of garment bags filled with keepsakes, including my oldest sister's prom-queen formal, my mother's wedding dress, and less-precious apparel such as dresses waiting to be passed down to whichever sibling was next in line or first to match an item's size. And there in the middle of the room, surrounded by the vestiges of a family's twentysome years together, sat the round, gray-and-white canister vacuum cleaner that I was looking for.

I moved forward into the room, but managed to take only one step before I froze in mid-stride. My approach was abbreviated by a sudden blaring noise. The sound was coming from the vacuum cleaner.

Staring wide-eyed at the appliance, I listened to the building roar of the vacuum cleaner's motor. In seconds, it leveled off to a steady whine, then stopped as abruptly as it had started.

I bolted out of the storeroom and back down the flight of stairs. Stunned and confused by what had happened, I frantically searched through the rooms on the main floor of the house, looking for my sisters. I was hoping that the sight of another person would relieve my fright. I finally found someone when I reached the kitchen.

"Betty, the vacuum cleaner in the storeroom started up by itself," I poured out in one continuous breath. "I heard it running. Really, I did."

My sister observed me for a moment, her eyes communicating skepticism and intolerance in a combined look that often appears on the faces of older siblings. Then she mumbled, "That's ridiculous. You must have heard something else."

Seconds later, I was standing alone in the kitchen, thinking that it would be a waste of my time to debate the issue. What I was saying was unbelievable. Still, I knew what I had heard, and mistaking the sound of a vacuum cleaner—its motor churning at an irritating decibel level—for some other noise was not what happened. What I heard *was* the vacuum cleaner.

There was something else about that incident, though, that even I found hard to believe: the vacuum cleaner wasn't even plugged in. The upstairs storeroom lacked any electrical outlets, and while the vacuum cleaner was running, the appliance's electrical cord was haphazardly coiled on the floor, the pronged end approximately ten inches from my feet.

Weeks would pass before I could walk into that storage room without feeling the grip of panic close down over my mind. And I kept my eye on that canister vacuum cleaner, half-believing that it was possessed by some demon that might cause it to act on its own again. Aside from that idea, the incident basically left me baffled, and I never came up with a sound explanation for what happened.

From that point forward in time, though, I never stuck my fingers into an electric blender, whether it was plugged into an outlet or not, nor did I place myself in the path of large, unattended machinery. My one experience with the vacuum cleaner was enough to convince me that certain principles that were supposed to define the world around me in a predictable way could no longer be trusted. Other paranormal experiences—though none as traumatic as the "vacuum cleaner" incident—would periodically occur to sustain that mistrust.

For instance, on a few occasions lightbulbs found a way of turning on or off without the normal flipping of a switch. A quick sweep of my hand near the base of a lamp or simply passing under a streetlight was all that seemed necessary to activate or deactivate these light sources. I was never trying to make the lights go on or off. In fact, whenever such peculiar anomalies happened, I was usually focused on some trivial matter. In one situation, I was simply reaching for the telephone, intending to place a call, when the bulb in the lamp on the phone stand suddenly lit up.

The only time I was ever aware of a connection between my thought processes and an unexplained event was on the evening of October 3, 1992. I had been watching television, but turned off the set around 11:00. In the middle of performing my usual bedtime routine, I decided that some background music would help to fill the silence.

I walked into my bedroom and headed toward the night table, intending to turn on the radio. My hand was about six inches from the clock-radio when I heard a mixture of voices and music coming from the living room.

I discovered that the television set had come on by itself. The background noise I consciously desired had mysteriously been provided, but I had intended that the source be the radio, not the TV.

Of course, in a technological age where wireless remote controls can sometimes trigger the on-off switches of distant appliances, perhaps this was not such an abnormal occurrence. But, during the five years in which I had owned that television, the set had never before come on by itself. I didn't even have a remote control for the television.

Without a firm rationale for why my television performed as it did, aside from an eerie sense that I had somehow willed it to switch on, I had no choice but to add the episode to my list of unexplained incidents. A short while later, though, I was reminded of an explanation that had come from the alien consciousness.

During the conversation that took place between the alien and I on the day I was sitting on the couch meditating about the nature of souls, I specifically asked her to explain the cause of the electrical disturbances I had witnessed in my life. She had offered an explanation, but I had forgotten all about that part of our conversation until I happened to see it again while paging through the notes I had taken.

"These incidents are self-directed," she had said. "It is your energy that initiates the activation of devices that power the mechanisms within. Be careful how you direct your energy. One day you will understand how this is possible. But today, this information would be too tempting to exploit."

Her inference that I would exploit such information was an insult. Proving that she was directly in touch with my mind and my emotions, she immediately added, "Don't think you are above such demonstrations. We've seen the actions of others more advanced in their awareness of their powers. Power is a dangerous tool in a world founded on the impressions of self rather than the pure energy of the body or species form."

The alien consciousness had punctuated her ending comment with an attitude that I had perceived before. It evoked in me the same feeling that accompanied the aliens' words during my hypnosis sessions. It was a form of condescension, a haughtiness that seemed to say, "You humans are like wild animals. Your focus on your individual selves makes you dangerous."

Reviewing my notes from that earlier conversation also reminded me of something the light beings had said during my hypnosis session regarding my purpose in the aliens' experiment. "You are like a satellite," they had told me, "radiating light as the sun. Balance...keeping energy in balance." Perhaps the alien consciousness and I were keeping each other in balance, and when our different energies, our separate consciousnesses, were unbalanced, we could perform some rather amazing tricks—though I was sure that such activities were not appropriate for the physical world.

While reading Kenneth Ring's *The Omega Project,* I learned that a large percentage of people reporting UFO encounters and alien abductions had also experienced a wide array of psychic phenomena throughout their lives. For some individuals, extrasensory perception or ESP—in the form of telepathy and precognition—and other paranormal activity such as psychokinesis had been present in their lives since childhood. Some abductees were even able to mark the beginning of their psychic abilities around the time of their first UFO sighting or alien contact.

I was fascinated by the relationship between alien encounters and paranormal activity. My interest prompted me to purchase the book *Parapsychology: The Controversial Science*, by Richard S. Broughton, Ph.D. I hoped that it would shed some light on the curious phenomena that occasionally manifested in my life.

Broughton, a parapsychologist, discussed current psychic research and recent theories and developments in the field of parapsychology. He also examined reincarnation, psychokinesis, ghosts, and the use of psychics in criminal investigations. The topic that I found most interesting, though, was a phenomenon known as remote viewing: the psychic observation of people, places, and things at a distance. Remote-viewing experimentation trials conducted under controlled laboratory conditions had netted positive results. The various parapsychology research institutions performing the trials found their results to be significant, enough to stand as evidence in support of ESP.

But how was it possible to "see" people, places, and things without physically being present? Exploring that question brought to mind my experiences during hypnosis. I had been "seeing" and interacting with life forms in some distant place. But it was my consciousness—actually my dual consciousness—that was standing with the aliens and the light beings in another realm.

I was intrigued by the phenomenon of remote viewing and how it could explain my vivid experiences during my hypnosis sessions. But I still questioned whether or not remote viewing was actually possible.

It seemed as if someone had been reading my mind because one day my question was answered, and whoever had been monitoring my inner musings had decided to offer me a personal glimpse into my own remote-viewing abilities.

When my "lesson" occurred, autumn was only days away. The weather, though, still resembled summer, producing warm, and humid temperatures that on this particular day in September had spawned a thick cover of gray clouds.

I stood at my kitchen counter, mixing together the ingredients for a vegetable quiche. Occasionally, I would glance through the window panels on the back door in the kitchen to catch displays of distant lightning and view the thunderclouds moving in from the northwest.

By the time I slid the quiche into the oven, a soft rain had begun to fall, and a damp breeze was drifting in through the open window above the kitchen sink. Rumblings of faraway thunder were carried on the breeze, as well as the faint sound of water droplets splashing against the leaves on the nearby trees.

The sound of the falling rain and the dropping air temperature inspired the idea of coffee, and just as I finished pouring water into my automatic drip coffeemaker, a brilliant flash of lightning sliced through my view from the kitchen window. A loud crack of thunder instantly followed, and my body jumped into the air.

The almost spontaneous combination of lightning and thunder foretold its location, and I suspected that if the electrical discharge had actually touched ground, it probably struck something nearby. Looking out the window, I searched through the trees and scanned the houses down the street for signs of possible lightning damage. Everything appeared to be fine.

I thought it was odd for lightning to suddenly strike my particular area, because there hadn't been any previous thunderclaps heard in the vicinity. The storm was still moving in. I was about to shift my attention back to making coffee when an unidentified voice broke through the quiet returning to my mind.

"That was for your benefit," I heard someone say. The voice carried a distinct quality and a masculine tone.

Maybe it was just the shock of hearing a disembodied voice that caused this, but it seemed as if time were being sucked out of the room, drawn down into some vacuous void. That sensation left me no choice but to stand completely still.

When the shock finally dissipated, time again moved forward. But rooted in my awareness was the sense that something extraordinary had just happened. Still, I found myself doubting what I had heard.

The voice that broke into my thoughts did not belong to the alien consciousness. Her conscious energy was softer, more feminine, which was why I regarded her as female. Whoever was holding conference with my mind had a masculine energy, and that entity was still there.

"What was for my benefit?" I asked, still feeling unsettled by the unexpectedness of the event.

A stream of information then shot into my awareness, and after it congealed into a recognizable impression, I realized that the entity was referring to the lightning I had seen just moments before.

"Oh, so you can control the weather, too," I said, forcing sarcasm into my words. "Leave me alone. I'm trying to make coffee here."

My sarcastic tone was really only a pretense meant to disguise my insecurities. That was just a human reaction, though, and a worthless one. The consciousness speaking to me was already in contact with my mind and my emotions.

At that moment, though, I was feeling intimidated by the ease in which the unidentified intelligence had stepped into my awareness. The power demonstrated by that act accentuated my humanness, my vulnerability. A part of me, too, was struggling to get out from under the sticky web of fear that had dropped down over me when I realized I was again in the presence of the unknown.

I wanted to resurrect the old denial that had once been an effective shield against the unseen entities and bizarre, nameless forces that occasionally crossed my path. Disavowing my own perceptions, though, hardly seemed appropriate for the situation. I couldn't deny that I heard a voice address me from out of the blue; I heard what I heard. Besides, I told myself, it was unlikely that doubt and denial would have any effect on making the entity go away if it wanted to speak to me. If this disembodied intelligence really had the power to send forth a bolt of lightning to get my attention, who was I to say that it didn't exist? I was still puzzling over the fact that the lightning flash and companion thunder seemed out of sync with the location of the storm. Maybe the entity *had* orchestrated that atmospheric phenomenon for my benefit.

As I considered the implications, I decided I had better change my attitude, and quickly, too, before the entity felt it necessary to display any more of its powers. I presented a show of genuine humility by "raising the white flag" with a mental message to declare my willing participation. "Who are you?" I asked. "What do you want?"

I took a couple of steps toward the middle of the kitchen, then stopped to search my mind for the stranger's response. A jumble of words, concepts and emotions were found there, swirling in a brew of shared consciousness. But the mixture lacked clarity; I couldn't comprehend the entity's meaning. Whatever information the entity was sending me just wasn't coming through. Then from out of the confusion came the entity's voice again.

"Lie down on your bed and relax," it said in a calm, but authoritative manner. "Clear your mind. Then you will understand."

Any doubt that I was actually dealing with some kind of intelligence completely washed away when I heard the voice a second time. And this time it filled me with awe rather than apprehension.

A gentleness wrapped around me for a moment, and a hint of familiarity filled my awareness. I wondered if the voice belonged to a light being. That impression quieted my fears and soothed my insecurities. Suddenly, I knew that the entity meant me no harm. It simply was there to show me something.

"What do I have to lose?" I silently voiced the words.

I glanced at the quiche baking in the oven, then walked out of the kitchen and toward the direction of my bedroom. Once there, I lay down on the bed and emptied my mind. Still, part of me wanted to say, "This is so stupid. I can't believe I'm actually obliging this guy." But after a couple of minutes, I started to see images forming in my mind.

It was like watching a movie, an action film, because the scene before my closed eyes depicted movement, wild activity. Although I wasn't actually hearing sounds, somewhere within my realm of perception I sensed the sounds of voices shouting, engines whirring, and rain falling. I could see a man, clad in dark-colored rain gear and a broad-brimmed hat, standing in the foreground. The man was waving his arms in a manner that suggested he was directing someone toward a specific location, as if directing traffic. While he performed that action, tiny fountains of rain splashed off the sleeves of his raincoat.

In the background, several yards behind the man, I vaguely detected a vehicle that looked like heavy road equipment. When I mentally concentrated on that part of the scene, it sharpened into focus. The vehicle in the distance was a fire truck. The bustle, the intense excitement, and the serious mood associated with the images flashing before my mind's eye suddenly made perfect sense: an emergency situation was unfolding, apparently a fire. Finally, the plot of my odd "movie" had been revealed.

Darkness gradually filled the screen before my eyes. When I finally opened them and centered myself again in my physical, three-dimensional world, I suddenly remembered that I had something baking in the oven.

Back in the kitchen, I checked on the progress of the quiche, crouching low toward the floor to peer through the glass window of the oven door. While sitting back on my heels, admiring the deep shades of amber spreading out across the surface of the egg mixture, the light above the kitchen sink suddenly came on.

The sudden change in the room's brightness yanked my attention toward the light. I stood up and stared at the space above the sink. "What is going on here?" I asked myself, aware that an icy chill was spreading over my body. This new curiosity, combined with the strange voice I had heard only minutes before, cast a supernatural glow over my reality.

I wondered if the entity who had spoken to me earlier was now playing tricks. Was it still trying to get my attention? Did it have something else to say?

The switch for the light above the sink was in the "on" position, and I reminded myself that that particular light had been turning on and off by itself over the past several months. Whenever it went off, a gentle tap on the recessed electrical housing usually made it come back on, suggesting that perhaps there was a bad connection in the wiring. Since the light had been switched on earlier, prior to my going into the bedroom, I assumed that it probably had gone off after that time. With this logic, I concluded that it wasn't really unnatural for the light to suddenly come on; the incident could be explained.

But then something else happened to challenge all logic.

I noticed that there wasn't any coffee in the coffeemaker's carafe. For a moment, I just assumed that I hadn't switched it on, thinking that the thunder and lightning and the arresting sound of a voice speaking into my head had diverted my attention. But while my eyes were locked onto the coffeemaker, dark brown water started to drip down into the carafe.

The coffeemaker was suddenly brewing coffee.

I could only shake my head in amazement. Evidently, the coffeemaker had been turned on prior to the sudden burst of lightning. But why hadn't it started brewing while I was still in the kitchen?

I thought that perhaps the lightning had caused the electricity to go off. But if it had, there would have been evidence of an electrical outage. I glanced at the microwave's digital display. Since the digits weren't flashing, I knew the electricity had not gone off at any time. The microwave was also plugged into the same electrical circuit as the coffeemaker. It could not have been an isolated problem, such as a blown fuse.

I had no way to explain why the electricity supplying the coffeemaker and the light over the kitchen sink had been temporarily interrupted. It seemed as if, from the moment of the lightning, a thin slice of reality had been lifted out of time.

I sipped coffee while watching the rain through the kitchen window. But I wasn't thinking about the rain. I was thinking about a question that was turning over and over again in my mind: Why did the entity want me to see the fire scene that unfolded before my closed eyes?

Over the next few hours, I got involved in other household projects and stopped thinking about the unknown voice and the meaning behind the fire scene. But it all came flooding back when I turned on the television to watch the early evening news.

There on the television screen was the scene I had witnessed while relaxing on my bed. A church located several blocks from my house had been struck by lightning. A fire had developed, and a news station had sent a camera crew to capture the event. Fire trucks had quickly arrived at the scene to manage the blaze.

The entity's voice saying, "That was for your benefit," echoed through my mind. "Okay. Okay. I get it," I said, hoping the entity might still be within reach. "Remote viewing is possible. You didn't have to blast a church with lightning to prove the point. You could have simply told me."

I really hoped that the connection between the lightning, the entity's words, the pictures I had seen in my mind, and the real fire that had started only blocks away was only a coincidence. Yet, it was difficult for me to see it as anything other than a lesson in paranormal phenomena that had been facilitated by an invisible instructor. My teacher, whoever he was, had set up an unusual demonstration to answer my questions about remote viewing.

Unexplained events continued to nudge me toward believing that forces from outside the physical boundaries of earth were ever present in my world. These forces seemed determined to further my education in dimensional physics.

The alien consciousness who was observing and experiencing my physical reality was also on hand from time to time to remind me that my world was not a private place. And it was always fascinating to discover what things in my reality caught her attention and prompted her to speak into my mind.

While standing in a grocery check-out lane, I saw a headline on the cover of the September 1992 issue of *Life* magazine that read "The Search for the Real E.T." The subhead, running along the edge of a dazzling, star-filled photograph of the Horsehead Nebula, posed the ultimate cosmic question: "Is there intelligent life in outer space?"

"Why do they still wonder?" issued the inner voice of the alien consciousness.

"I don't know why," I answered back telepathically.

I stepped closer to the magazine rack to read the entire subhead: "Is there intelligent life in outer space? A $100 million NASA program, beginning this fall, may finally answer one of mankind's most compelling questions."

As I read those words, the edges of my lips curled upward. To an onlooker, it might have appeared that I was smiling. But the expression on my face was really a smirk, and not even my own.

It was the alien's reaction to the U.S. government's willingness to spend 100 million dollars in an effort to scan the noise coming from outer space with aspirations of finding evidence that intelligent life is "out there." From the alien's perspective, that effort seemed humorously embryonic.

The physical realm was not the only place where my lessons in the outer limits of reality were being taught. My dreams continued to take me to strange places. My instruction there was always remarkable, sometimes even extraordinary, and alien beings continued to show up in my dream life, too.

During the night of October 31, 1992, I woke into a dreamscape where I was having a difficult time keeping my feet on the ground. I was walking outdoors at night in an unfamiliar place, when without any warning I was lifted into the air by some unseen force. I found myself soaring through space without the aid of any mechanical device. It seemed as though I blanked out for a period of time, and when my awareness returned, I was about 100 feet above the ground, looking down on a most peculiar sight.

Alien bodies were scattered on the terrain below me. There were perhaps twenty or more in my view. And scurrying around their grayish white forms were human beings. Somehow I knew was looking at the crash site of an alien spaceship.

Seconds later, I was standing in a building that carried the ambiance of a lodge or a country resort. At first I was in a large room with vaulted ceiling, a huge fireplace, knotty-pine paneling on the ceiling and the walls, and rustic furnishings. After scanning my surroundings, my curiosity sent me exploring in another direction.

I found a group of about thirty or forty men and women gathered together in two connecting rooms. They were mingling as people do at a social gathering. I knew that they had been brought to the lodge for a very specific purpose, yet I doubted if the men and women were aware of what was expected of them. I took it upon myself to share the news.

"Do you all know why you're here?" I asked, shouting out my question in order to be heard above the drone of voices. "Listen to me. Do you know why you're here?"

About half of the people looked up at me, and the noise level in the area dropped off significantly, allowing me to ask my next question without having to raise my voice. "How many of you have a medical degree or have a medical background?"

Three-fourths of the people in the room raised their hands. An array of quizzical expressions swept across their faces.

I walked into the adjoining room and asked the same question. Everyone in the smaller room raised a hand. But before I could explain to the men and women standing around me that they had been brought to the lodge as a medical team to assist in the emergency treatment of a group of aliens whose aircraft had crashed nearby, I was pulled up from where I was standing, as if I were a marionette and the puppeteer had decided to quickly end the show.

Within seconds, I was rising toward the ceiling in the lodge's main room, seeing the floor rapidly drop away beneath my feet. When I reached the peak of the vaulted ceiling, I fastened my hands around a black metal pipe that stretched across the center of the ceiling in an effort to prevent myself from being pulled through the roof. I managed to hold on to the pipe for a few seconds, but the invisible force controlling my body outmatched my physical strength, and then I melted into the knotty-pine paneling.

The sensation of moving through solid objects was not a new experience for me. I could remember being pulled through a wall once before, while navigating space during another strange dream. That particular dream occurred long before I was aware of my involvement in the alien abduction phenomenon.

In that dream, I was flying through the night sky, just above the skyline of a large city. Tall buildings were passing beneath me as

I floated over their rooftops. When I lifted my head to look in the direction of my flight, I saw a huge skyscraper coming up fast. Since I was not in control of my body and had no idea who was, panic bit down over my mind. I thought I was about to slam into the side of the building.

I closed my eyes just seconds before impact, but instead of hitting the wall, I painlessly passed into the structure. What I saw when I opened my eyes was amazing. I was looking at the physical composition of the wall while moving through it. A tight, translucent grid pattern appeared before my eyes, and it filled the visible space around me. I moved through layer after layer of what should have been solid material until I was on the other side of the building and back out in the night air.

Toward the end of January 1993, I had another dream that involved moving through walls. Again, I woke into the night and into the outdoors. I was standing in the outer fringe of a large group of strangers and on a platform or some sort of balcony that was at least thirty feet across and thirty feet wide. I walked over to the metal railing that circled the edge of the platform to get a fix on my location. When I looked over the railing, I discovered that I was at least five or six stories above the ground.

I spent the next few minutes trying to determine where I was and the purpose of the gathering. Somewhere within my awareness, I had the sense that we were going to leave soon and travel to another location.

What I remembered next was being inside a house. The walls of this structure were also covered with knotty-pine paneling, similar to the walls in the lodge that I had visited in another dream. This house, though, was much smaller than the country lodge.

I was standing in an area that opened up into a living room and a dining area that was adjacent to a kitchen. Above the living space was a second-story loft that stretched across the entire length of the living room. An older woman with long, graying hair was standing up in the loft looking down at me.

No words were being spoken, yet the woman was definitely communicating her thoughts. I could hear them in my mind, and she was saying, "Leave now. Go and practice what you have learned." I knew that her lesson had been on how to walk through walls and transport myself through space.

My perception shifted, and then it seemed as though I were observing reality from inside another person's body. The individual who now mastered my physical form was the one who had been instructed in the secret of walking through solid objects. I had no knowledge of that skill. I remember moving across the room and seeing the wall in front of me getting closer and closer until I stepped right through it and into the wintry night. I floated through the air several feet above the ground, scanning the grounds from an aerial position.

The terrain immediately below me was covered with snow, and off to my right was a frozen pond. Three snow sculptures that varied in size from small, medium, to large were positioned near the edge of the pond. I stared at them for a short time, trying to determine what they represented, but I was too far above the ground to make sense of their shapes. A few miles off in the distance, I could see hundreds of dots of light—obviously a small city.

Everything around me was fascinating, and the panorama before my eyes was truly a spectacular view. But in the back of my mind, I kept thinking that I was supposed to be practicing my flying. That thought kept coming in and out of my mind until I suddenly felt myself being pulled up into the air. I was in the grip of an unseen power, and the feeling that surged through my body and my mind in that instant told me that I was in the hands of my Others—the light beings.

The overwhelming bliss, the joy, the rapture that I had experienced while standing with the light beings during my first hypnosis session filled my mind and my soul once again. It swelled inside me as I went farther and farther up into the air. I watched the snow-covered scene shrink below me, my face beaming with happiness as I connected with my Others. When I woke from sleep in the morning, that harmonious blend of emotion was still deep within my heart.

Nothing of note—at least in the sense of alien encounters or paranormal activity or bizarre dreams—occurred during the next four months. Then, on May 28, 1993, my gray friends, the little gray guys, my alien buddies—new names I had given the aliens—showed up in my life again. I'm not certain if they abducted me during their, but I'm sure they took my younger sister, Lori.

Lori and I had packed up our bicycles and our camping gear at the start of the Memorial Day weekend and drove to Tunnel Trail Campground near Wilton, Wisconsin. We planned to explore the Elroy-Sparta State Bike Trail.

We arrived at the campground in the early evening. Our campsite was tucked back behind a narrow strip of woods and it was bordered on the opposite side by a huge grass-covered knoll. In comparison to the other campsites, our location was definitely the most isolated area within the entire campground.

We quickly put up our tent in the fading outdoor light then built a fire. We sat at our picnic table, eating things we didn't need to cook, until we grew tired. It was probably close to 11:30 p.m. by the time Lori and I crawled into our sleeping bags.

Our tent was designed to sleep six people, so we had plenty of room for the queen-sized air mattress that kept us up off the cold, hard ground. Yet, in spite of conditions that should have permitted a comfortable rest, I kept waking up during the night, feeling chilled. Even though my sleeping bag was meant for cool temperatures, I just couldn't snuggle deep enough into the flannel lining to stay warm.

My sister appeared to be sleeping peacefully. I would glance over at her form whenever I woke up. Lori's mummy bag was zipped up over her head, and she was tucked deep inside.

The first two times I woke up during the night, I found her lying next to me on the inflated mattress. But the third time, I discovered that her sleeping bag was empty. The mound that had been Lori's body was gone.

I thought that she had gotten up to go to the bathroom. Yet, that didn't make sense to me, because I knew I would have heard her moving around in the tent. I picked my head up off my pillow to look toward the bottom of the air mattress, thinking that perhaps Lori had somehow turned her body around.

Lori's head and upper torso were in view, and it looked like she was out of her sleeping bag and leaning against something. Or was it someone? She was facing me, but slumped over, her head cocked to one side with her chin resting against her chest. It seemed odd to me that she would be sleeping in that awkward position. What was even stranger was the impression I had that what I was seeing was occurring somewhere else, somewhere other than inside the tent.

I dropped my head back down on the pillow and searched through my mind for an explanation. The image of my sister was stuck there; it didn't make any sense. How could she be propped up like that when there isn't anything to lean against in the tent? How did she get turned around? Why is her sleeping bag empty? Why did I think that she was leaning against someone?

I was about to raise my head again and take another look, but I heard a voice in my head saying, "Just go back to sleep. You don't want to look again."

But I wanted to look again, and I tried to pick my head up off the pillow. I tried really hard. Yet, I wasn't able to do it. That was the last thing I remembered from the night.

In the morning, I found my sister lying exactly where she had been earlier in the night, in her sleeping bag, with her face again barely a foot away from my own.

When Lori woke up, I asked her if she had gotten up during the night or if she had switched her sleeping position at any time. She assured me that she hadn't moved from her sleeping bag, then added that she hadn't slept very well. "I just couldn't get warm enough," she said. "I woke up on and off during the night because I was cold."

I described to my sister what I had observed during the night, and we had a good laugh about it. Lori was aware of my alien abduction experiences, and the idea that the aliens had taken her instead of me was amusing to her. Having no memory of a disturbance in the tent, Lori easily dismissed the whole episode.

Almost a year before, I had asked her if she could recall anything in her life that might be related to the alien abduction phenomenon. The only connection she could make was a dream she once had in which she saw a spaceship hovering over a field near the farm in Wisconsin where we both grew up. If she was involved in the phenomenon, she certainly wasn't remembering her experiences. With that being the case, she saw no need to explore the matter any further.

Our second night in the tent went by uneventfully. Lori and I had no problem staying warm inside our sleeping bags, though the air temperature was not much different than the temperature during the evening before. We both slept solidly, too. Of course, we had biked over forty miles during the day, which might have explained why we didn't wake up very often during the night.

My first night back in Minneapolis, and back in my own bed, produced another strange and perhaps telling dream-like experience. Though most of the dream's details were blurred by morning. All I could remember was standing next to a table, along with several other forms whose faces and bodies were no longer definable. The only clear memory that I brought with me into the morning was my angry voice lambasting the people near the table. I was mad, but in a subdued sort of way, and telling the people standing next to me that they shouldn't have brought my sister Lori, who was lying on the table, to the place where we were.

Maybe it was only a dream, but then, maybe not. Maybe I had remembered that scene from the night when Lori disappeared from the tent. Maybe the aliens had abducted me, too, and both Lori and I had disappeared into the aliens' dimensional world.

Only one unusual incident marked the month of June. I lost about an hour on my digital clock-radio that sat on the night table next to my bed. The electricity had not gone off in the house, nor had I changed the settings on the clock. And even if I had accidentally bumped the buttons that changed the time setting, the time showing on the clock would have moved forward, not backward. All the other clocks in the house were still set at the appropriate time. Yet the clock next to my bed was nearly an hour behind, and that had never happened before.

By the summer of 1993, I had become acclimated to the unexpected, the unusual and the unknown. But what took place during the early hours of July 1, 1993, would crown my list of strange and extraordinary incidents.

What happened that night rocked my world once again, shaking even the newly laid foundation that I had set down as my expanded reality. But instead of splitting the ground wide open with fear, this particular incident proved to me that over the course of two years I had changed. No longer was I a woman terrified of the night. Instead, I was a human being willing to reach out and take the next step toward communicating with the aliens who insisted on straying into my world.

My bedroom door was locked that night, and I was alone in my house. I had left a light on in my bedroom, since soft lamplight had become for me what a pacifier is to a baby. I needed the light to feel secure, I needed it to fall asleep.

During the night, I came up into consciousness and into a strange situation. I was lying on my left side, near the center of the bed. My right arm was draped over a thick feather pillow that was tucked lengthwise along the front of my body. I could feel my elbow and lower arm resting on the pillow, but my hand was not touching the bed. It was slightly elevated above the mattress, and my fingers were resting across a unique surface that I knew was a stranger's hand.

They're here again, I thought. The aliens are back, and one of them is holding my hand.

I wasn't half-asleep or still coming up out of sleep. I felt as if I were completely awake, fully conscious of everything happening in the room.

My eyes were closed, but I sensed several beings standing next to the bed. My impression was that three small forms were in front of me and at least two were at the foot of the bed. I also sensed two or three other beings standing behind me, positioned on the other side of the room. It was an extraordinary feeling, being surrounded like that.

I kept my eyes closed and stayed absolutely still. My mind, though, was tracking every second. I was contemplating a risky move and waiting for the right moment to act. I wanted to see the aliens. I wanted to open my eyes and look at the beings standing next to my bed. I wanted to experience their physical appearance with all of my senses.

I heard a voice inside my mind say, "Are you ready to do this?" But I wasn't sure if the words were coming from me or someone else.

I briefly regarded the question, yet decided to take the leap. But nothing happened when I commanded my eyelids to lift. My eyes wouldn't open. Disappointment filled my consciousness, as I waited for something to happen.

I think the aliens were reading my thoughts and, as if to say, *We can't allow you to open your eyes, but we will permit you to touch us*, I suddenly was able to move my right hand. Using my fingers, I began exploring the hand that was gently supporting my own.

The alien's hand was hard, and it felt small, too, like a child's hand, though the stiff and bony fingers were proportionately longer and narrower. I carefully slid my human flesh across the top portion of the alien's outstretched hand until my fingers folded over its outer edge. My thumb and index finger selected the outer digit on the alien's hand and explored its length, all the way down to the tapered end where my thumb made an unexpected find. At the tip was something like a fingernail, but the arched contour of the nail caused me to think that I was touching a claw.

As the reality of the alien's nonhuman form sank in, a question blazed up in my mind: *My God, what is at the other end of this hand? What do these beings really look like?* Then fear flooded my consciousness. Abruptly, the alien withdrew its hand, and mine plopped down onto the bed.

Within seconds of separating from the alien, the beings in the room began communicating with me telepathically. They were explaining something that I basically understood to mean that they were going to take me someplace.

My fear immediately rose to the level of panic. Then my consciousness began performing some strange routine. I felt as if I were suddenly flying upward toward a door through which I could escape. A part of me was frantically moving up through a vertical tunnel, but at the speed of light. When I reached the top, I had to break through a thin layer that covered the surface, like the first ice on a pond.

Whatever that layer was, it seemed to be responsible for the physical paralysis still binding my body. Smashing through it freed my muscles, and I opened my eyes and sat up in bed.

The small lamp that I had left on in my bedroom enabled me to see that the room was empty. The aliens were gone. I looked over at my clock-radio to check the time. It was 1:14 a.m.

My heart was pounding, but the fear and panic were quickly fading away. It seemed to me that I'd just experienced a miracle.

"They let me touch them," I said. "They actually let me touch them." I repeated those words over and over until the reality had settled.

I felt stunned, physically and psychically. First, by the fact that the aliens allowed the human "me" to remain conscious during the encounter, and secondly, by the way they had attempted to interact with that part of me. They hadn't exactly asked for my permission, but they did at least tell me of their intention to take me out of my bedroom.

Unfortunately, I panicked. But if the strange beings had been tracking my thoughts during the encounter, they would have learned that claws, even claw-like fingernails, can make a human more than uncomfortable: they can generate fear. I hoped that I hadn't given the beings the impression that a human would find their bodies too repulsive to look at. On the other hand, while the aliens stood around the bed looking down on my human face, they might have been thinking that I was the one who looked hideous.

The encounter did confirm for me—and certainly for the aliens—that I wasn't ready to look at their physical form with my human eyes. Yet, I wondered if the aliens were preparing me for that experience by allowing me to "see" aspects of their bodies in my mind through touch before actually permitting the full view.

My memory of the gray, alien face, witnessed as a teenager, was probably the clearest image I had of an actual alien. I had, of course, frequently viewed alien forms during hypnosis and as memories from dream-like encounters. But I couldn't remember a time when I had actually perceived their entire bodies with my human awareness, that I was looking at an alien life form. Even the encounter that took place in my parents' bedroom during childhood was first thought to be a dream.

Following the aliens' sudden exit from my room, I just sat on my bed, reflecting on what had happened. But I soon noticed something odd. My bedroom door and the wood molding around it appeared to be covered with a grayish-white film. I scanned the room to check the color of other objects, but everything else appeared normal. Even the closet doors that matched the material and stain of the bedroom door were unchanged. After about ten minutes, the gray film on the door faded, and the door returned to its original color.

I had never observed that phenomenon in my room before, but after that night, there were other times when I would wake up and find that my bedroom door was again wearing that grayish white film. Once I even climbed out of bed and walked over to the door to run my hand across its surface. I expected to find a powdery substance, but found nothing covering the door. What I discovered was that the gray color was imbedded into the wood. It was as if the molecular structure of the door had been altered somehow, affecting the wood's appearance. Yet the door would always revert back to its original color, sometimes within seconds, other times within minutes.

I fought sleep for nearly an hour after the aliens' visit. Since I had foiled the aliens' attempt to abduct me, I expected the creatures to return. Sometime during the night, though, I must have fallen back asleep, because it was daylight when I looked around my bedroom again.

For a while that morning, I just sat on the edge of my bed, near the place where the alien had stood, the one who had held my hand, and cried. I wasn't crying out of fear or distress. I was crying because I was overwhelmed with emotion. I was amazed, excited, and still feeling stunned by what had happened in my bedroom during the night. I could still feel the alien's hand holding mine. I could still recall what it felt like as I explored the dimensions of its hard, bony surface. I could still feel the smooth arch of the alien's nail under my thumb. It was too much to comprehend, so I cried.

My attitude toward nonhuman life forms dramatically shifted after that night, and it began with a simple touch. Touch is a powerful medium, and being allowed to explore the small hand of the alien standing at my bedside conveyed trust. And the gentle way the alien held my hand conveyed affection. As my fingers roamed the surface of the alien's hand, an exchange took place. There was

intimate contact between two beings—one human, one alien—
coming together from dissimilar worlds.

After a lifetime of strange encounters, the peculiar alien beings
had finally permitted me to interact with them as a human being.
In spite of all I had experienced in the presence of aliens, that
reality was still staggering.

EPILOGUE

EXTRAORDINARY EXPERIENCE IS SOMETHING profound and transforming, though it often leaves the experiencer standing alone. It pen-
etrates your beliefs, values, and attitudes, going right to the core,
to expose every possible vulnerability that exists within you.
You're no longer like everyone else, no longer just part of the
crowd. And there you are, naked with your truth, wondering if
you should step forward, while knowing that your vulnerabilities
may destroy you. It's not an easy choice to share extraordinary
experience with the world.

The alien abduction phenomenon is all about extraordinary
experience. On the surface, it wears a chameleon-like façade, but
when you look deeper, it really isn't all that mysterious. It's just
extraordinary, different, unique—that is, to humans. To understand it requires an equally unique perspective. My father captured that perspective best when, at the end of a long
conversation during which I attempted to explain to my parents

my involvement in the alien abduction phenomenon, he said, "You sure live in a different world than the one I live in."

My father's words, though far from comforting, smacked of the truth. In my world, even the laws of physics are no longer true. Walls become vapor, time flips on its side, locked doors are delusions of safety, and sometimes I can fly. Even electrical appliances are unpredictable. I do live in a different world from my parents and from most of my friends. And many of my life experiences have truly been unconventional, even bizarre. But I am learning to cope with the extraordinary experiences in my life as best I can. I have no other choice. I know now that living in the presence of aliens has always been my choice.

Fortunately, living within the shadow of aliens and strange phenomena has slowly taken on a brighter cast over time. The thick haze of fear that once blackened my nights has finally lifted and I've learned to live with the uncertainty in my life. That is not to say that the fear and the anxiety went away quickly. There were still many nights when I would practically jump out of sleep and feel the quickening of my heart as my eyes searched around my bedroom. I just got better at convincing myself that I had nothing to fear, and eventually I came to believe it.

Whenever the fear and anxiety did walk back into my life, I would remind myself of the light beings' words when Mr. Dallek prompted me to search for an answer that would allow me to get a good night's sleep. "Understand," the light beings had said. "Seek understanding in the light...as in the light in your room."

Just as a night light left on in my bedroom bathed me in a conscious glow of comfort and protection, the transformational power of standing in the light beings' radiance—if only in my mind— always elevated me above the fear that sometimes fogged over my sensibilities.

My new understanding around my spiritual origins and my agreement to participate in an alien culture's experiment also put my situation into a different light, creating a new perspective.

Recognizing that at some point in my eternal past I had agreed to live an unconventional human life for the sake of learning and to fulfill an alien's quest to experience the human condition somehow made it easier to face the night and the possibility that I would wake to find alien beings in my room again.

Over time, I even started to view my involvement with aliens and my relationship with the unknown as a valuable asset. What had once been only an annoying challenge, laced with nights of misery and emotional pain, gradually evolved to reveal the bright and friendly wrappings of a special gift. That gift was in the form of knowledge, of enlightenment, of spiritual truth.

As I further opened my mind and my soul to the dimensional beings who continued to walk through my walls, I came to realize that everything that was happening to me, in spite of its bizarre and baffling nature, was in fact the endowment of a new reality, a reality that was waiting for all humankind.

Realizing the truth and potential of that reality didn't come to me as a blast of sudden insight. It took months that turned into years of soul searching, study and meditation. Listening to the tape recording of my second hypnosis session two years after it occurred confirmed the time that had elapsed before I had come to understand certain concepts. Gary Dallek had actually explained aspects of dimensional realities quite well during my session, but I wasn't prepared at the time to grasp the deeper meaning. He had said, "So the things that go bump in the night, the things that come out of the woodwork, that simply shift from one dimension to another, they've been able to do that for quite a long time, as have many other beings, entities, energies, spiritual essences, or other dimensional knowledge. Seems like we're the last ones to know...But each human is a separate entity kind of locked into itself, locked into a process, yet very much still not aware of the greater whole. The transformation seems to be unlocking the consciousness into the greater whole...So what we're looking at is really the opening of human consciousness ..."

My extraordinary experiences eventually forced me to unlock rigid views and expectations about my human reality and open myself up to the greater whole, a broader, universal perspective. In response, I restructured my belief system. I now see the universe as a vast, multidimensional playground, filled with many beings, fascinating technologies, and unique modes of communication and travel. The human experience happens to be just one dimension of reality, a dimension in which nonhuman life forms are actively exploring.

The alien abduction phenomenon solidly supports the view that alien beings are interested in human psychology and biology, particularly our genetics and reproductive capabilities. Yet, it is clear to me that aliens are attempting to do more than just explore the basics of who we are. My experiences with alien life forms—though limited to the thin, gray aliens and the squat, dwarf-like brown-eyed beings—suggest to me that it is also within the aliens' charter to transform our limited "human" view of ourselves and to help us discover the dimensional universe. Alien life forms may actually be agents for planetary change. But why would alien life forms want us humans to change and broaden our perspectives and our beliefs?

Readiness, on the part of the student, is always a critical factor whenever new learning is to take place. Perhaps aliens and other dimensional life forms are helping humans evolve intellectually, emotionally, and spiritually in preparation for what is yet to come. Maybe we humans have some maturing to do before we can view our encounters with alien beings from the proper perspective: participant versus victim, communicator versus silent observer, and diplomat versus militant. Many human beings are rapidly evolving toward those directions now. Still, it may be important that we collectively change. Could it be that *all* humans must come to see themselves as cosmic cousins to life forms living on the flip side of human time and space before we are formally introduced?

I believe that aliens expect contact with humans on a grand level. They're obviously preparing *themselves* through research and study, even through the human experience.

In the meantime, are they simply waiting for us?

Endnotes

1 Budd Hopkins, *Missing Time*, (New York: Ballantine Books,1981), p. 60

2 Raymond E. Fowler, *The Watchers* (New York: Bantam Books, 1990), p. 176

3 Edith Fiore, Ph.D., *Encounters* (New York: Ballantine Books, 1989), pp. 67-68

4 Kenneth Ring, Ph.D., *The Omega Project* (New York: William Morrow and Company, Inc., 1992), p. 131

5 Budd Hopkins, *Intruders: The Incredible Visitations at Copley Woods* (New York: Random House, 1987), p. 135

6 Ring, *The Omega Project*, p. 71

7 Fiore, *Encounters*, pp. 15-16

8 Ring, *The Omega Project*, p. 52

9 Whitley Strieber, *Communion: A True Story* (New York: Beech Tree Books/William Morrow and Company, Inc., 1987), p. 24

10 Fiore, *Encounters*, p. 56

11 Strieber, *Communion*, p. 30

12 David M. Jacobs P.h.D., *Secret Life* (New York: Simon & Schuster, 1992), pp. 53-54

13 Strieber, *Communion*, p. 22

Stay in Touch. . .

Llewellyn publishes hundreds of books on your favorite subjects. On the following pages you will find listed some books now available on related subjects. Your local bookstore stocks most of these and will stock new Llewellyn titles as they become available. We urge your patronage.

Order by Phone

Call toll-free within the U.S. and Canada, 1–800–THE MOON.
In Minnesota call (612) 291–1970.
We accept Visa, MasterCard, and American Express.

Order by Mail

Send the full price of your order (MN residents add 7% sales tax) in U.S. funds to:

Llewellyn Worldwide
P.O. Box 64383, Dept. K063-9
St. Paul, MN 55164–0383, U.S.A.

Postage and Handling

- ◆ $4.00 for orders $15 and under
- ◆ $5.00 for orders over $15
- ◆ No charge for orders over $100

We ship UPS in the continental United States. We cannot ship to P.O. boxes. Orders shipped to Alaska, Hawaii, Canada, Mexico, and Puerto Rico will be sent first class mail.

International orders: Airmail—add freight equal to price of each book to the total price of order, plus $5.00 for each non-book item (audiotapes, etc.). Surface mail—Add $1.00 per item.

Allow 4–6 weeks delivery on all orders. Postage and handling rates subject to change.

Group Discounts

We offer a 20% quantity discount to group leaders or agents. You must order a minimum of 5 copies of the same book to get our special quantity price.

Free Catalog

Get a free copy of our color catalog, New Worlds of Mind and Spirit. Subscribe for just $10.00 in the United States and Canada ($20.00 overseas, first class mail). Many bookstores carry New Worlds—ask for it!